A STRAIGHTFORWARD GUIDE INDIVIDUAL AND FAMILY FINANCES

Adrian Fellowes

Straightforward Guides

Straightforward Guides

ISBN :

978-1-84716-503-9

Printed by Grosvenor Press

Cover design by Bookworks Islington

CONTENTS

INTRODUCTION

The main purpose of this book is to guide the reader through the maze of personal financial decisions which he or she or the family might have to make during a lifetime. During the severe recession, from which we are now emerging and after a prolonged period of low interest rates, savers and investors are now getting meager returns. That is why it is so important to understand the opportunities available.

I have concentrated heavily on specific areas such as pensions, savings and insurance, because these are areas which have undergone change following the recent 2015 budget in particular and which will have the most effect on you during the course of your working life. The book also discusses the operations of the stock market and how to invest wisely. There are also frequent references to financial advisors, ranging from the independent advisor to those employed by institutions such as banks. I have made repeated references because very often you will receive advice from such a person and will make decisions based on that advice.

As an individual, you could spend untold hours the various options open to you with regard to financial matters, only to find yourself more confused than ever due to conflicting advice received along the way. That advice will, quite often, be made in the best interests of the advisor, and his or her subsequent commissions, rather than in the best interests of yourself.

A Guide to Individual and Family Finances will set out, in a clear and unambiguous way, the meaning and implications of the various financial options open to you, and should leave you in a better position to make an informed choice.

The main areas covered by the book are mortgages, life insurance, savings, investments, income protection, stocks and shares, tax wills and trusts and pensions. In addition, I have covered education, health care, weddings and funerals.

Because of the importance of receiving accurate advice from financial advisors, the book will begin by outlining the law that governs such advisors and also the types of advice given.

****

1

Financial Advice and Financial Advisors

There are many ways to purchase financial products nowadays, either through the Internet or by telephone. However, when considering more complex financial issues, it is evident that professional advice is needed. There are numerous advantages to using financial advisors, one of the main ones being that you will have extra protection if things go wrong. The first step towards finding a good advisor is considering which type is likely to provide the service you need. Like solicitors and other professionals, financial advisors do specialise and you would have to find the correct advisor for your needs. It is also very important to discover whether or not the advisor is properly authorised and registered and approved by the correct bodies. Nowadays, advisors and the companies that they work for must be authorised by the financial services watchdog, the Financial Conduct Authority (FCA). The FCA is responsible for the conduct of advisors. To be on the safe side you should always check with the FCA. You can also find out what type of business the advisor is authorised to do. These details are held on the FCA's register. Its public enquiries helpline is on 0300 500 5957. It is important to be aware of the distinctions between different types of advisors, the services they are likely to provide, and how they are likely to be paid, before narrowing your choice down.

Different types of investment advisers

If you are getting advice about investing your money, you need to know there are two different types of financial advisers – 'independent' and 'restricted' – and this can affect the advice you are given. Some advisers can offer the full range of financial products and providers available, and are called 'independent advisers'. But many advisers have chosen to offer 'restricted advice' and will focus on a limited selection of products and/or providers.

All financial advisers have to be approved or authorised by the FCA.. Both independent and restricted advisers must pass the same qualifications and meet the same requirements to ensure they are providing suitable advice. An adviser or firm has to tell you in writing whether they offer independent or restricted advice, but if you are not sure which they offer you should ask for more information.

Independent advisers

An adviser or firm that provides independent advice is able to consider and recommend all types of retail investment products that could meet your needs and objectives. Independent advisers will also consider products from all firms across the market, and have to give unbiased and unrestricted advice. An independent adviser may also be called an 'independent financial adviser' or 'IFA'.

Restricted advisers

A restricted adviser or firm can only recommend certain products, product providers, or both. The adviser or firm has to clearly explain the nature of the restriction. If you are not sure you should ask for further information, but some examples of restricted advice are where:

- The adviser works with one product provider and only considers products that company offers.
- The adviser considers products from several – but not all – product providers.
- The adviser can recommend one or some types of products, but not all retail investment products.
- The adviser has chosen to focus on a particular market, such as pensions, and considers products from all providers within that market.

Restricted advisers and firms cannot describe the advice they offer as 'independent'.

Other types of 'advice'

If you are only given general information about one or more investment products, or have products or related terms explained to you, you may have received 'guidance' rather than 'advice'. This is sometimes also called an 'information only' or 'non-advice' service. The main difference between guidance and advice is that you decide which product to buy without having one or more recommended to you. Buying an investment product in this way might reduce the cost involved but it also means you might not have access to the Financial Ombudsman Service or Financial Services Compensation Scheme (FSCS) if things go wrong.

If you are not sure whether you are receiving guidance or advice, and therefore how you would be protected, you should ask the adviser or firm to explain.

See overleaf for summary of differences.

Independent and restricted advice: key differences

	Independent adviser	Restricted advisers
Will consider all retail investment products	Yes	No
Can focus only on a particular market	No	Yes
Can consider products only from certain product providers	No	Yes
Has to explain to you the type of advice they offer	Yes	Yes
Can use 'independent' to describe the advice they offer	Yes	No
Incentivised to recommend one product over another	No	No

Fees and charges

A financial adviser can help you make the most of your money but you need to be confident you are getting advice that is right for you. there have been improvements in this area. From 31 December 2012 the Retail Distribution Review (RDR) came into effect which means you:

1. Know how much advice costs

Advice has never been free. If you received financial advice before the changes you were probably paying commission to your adviser. Commission was usually a percentage of your investment – typically 1% to 8%, or sometimes more on a lump sum. So for an investment of £10,000, your adviser could have received between £100 and £800 commission.

Instead of you paying commission on new investments your adviser now has to clearly explain how much advice will cost and together you will agree how you will pay for it. This can be a set fee paid upfront or you may be able to agree with your adviser that they can take their fee from the sum you invest. This way you know exactly what you are paying and that the advice you receive is not influenced by how much your adviser could earn from the investment.

2. Know what you are paying for

Financial advisers can either advise you on all products that may be right for you or focus on certain areas, such as pensions.

Following the changes, financial advisers that provide 'independent' advice now have to consider all types of investment areas. They can also consider products from all firms across the market. An adviser that has chosen to offer 'restricted' advice can only consider certain products, product providers or both. Your adviser has to clearly explain what they can advise you on.

3. Get improved professional standards

Some investments can be hard to understand. So the FCA have increased the minimum professional standards of qualification that advisers have to meet, to ensure their knowledge is up to date.

What you should do next

Next time you see your adviser ask how much you have been paying for their advice and how much that same advice now costs. Your adviser should be able to explain how these changes affect you and your finances, and whether they offer independent or restricted advice.

Services offered by other advisers

Accountants

Accountants are usually the best source of advice on tax matters. Some can also advise on investments provided that they are authorised by the FCA. Some of the larger accountancy forms have specialist independent financial advice departments to provide a full planning service. You will have to pay a fee to accountants for such advice but any commission generated by sales of products is usually offset against the final bill.

For names of local accountants contact the Institute of Chartered Accountants, the Association of Chartered certified Accountants or the Chartered Institute of Taxation and Association of Tax Technicians (see appendix).

Actuaries

Actuaries are normally employed by insurance companies but there are also firms of independent consultants who can be approached for specialist advice on insurance related matters such as pension transfers. They work on a fee basis. The Association of Consulting Actuaries can provide you with the name of a firm in your area.

Banks and building societies

Most larger banks and building societies have in-house financial consultants who are tied agents. In the future, some banks may become multi-tied and start offering the products of several companies but their range will still remain limited. Some banks offer advice through private arms designed for wealthier customers (with more than £100,000 to invest for example).

Company representatives

Many insurance companies have their own sales forces to promote their products and services. Traditional insurers, such as Legal and General and the Co-operative still employ hundreds of representatives who will visit people in their own homes to discuss their needs.

Companies selling direct by telephone also use their own representatives.

Solicitors

If you need legal advice on certain matters such as dealing with wills and probate, you will need to consult a firm of solicitors. They may also be able to provide financial planning and investment advice on a fee basis. There are two organisations that represent solicitors offering these services. They are the Association of Solicitor Investment Managers (ASIM) and Solicitors for Independent Investment Advice. If you have a legal problem relating to a pension, you should contact the Association of Pension Lawyers. See appendix for details.

Stockbrokers

Stockbrokers have become more accessible over the years, particularly recently. Many of the newer telephone based services cater mainly for investors who know which shares they want to buy and sell, and they do not provide advice other than general information bulletins. However, many firms still offer advisory and discretionary management services. For smaller investors, a unit or investment manage trust management may be offered.

To find out which stockbrokers offer these services to private clients, contact the Association of Private Client Investment Managers and Stockbrokers (APCIMS). It has a free directory of member firms, many of which provide a full financial planning service. See appendix for details.

Tied agents

Tied agents are also known as 'appointed representatives'. These are self-employed consultants or companies, which have a contract to sell one or more of an insurance company's products or commission. The agent may operate independently in respect of other business. For example, many building societies are tied agents and will sell the investment and investment products of one insurance company.

Complaints

If you are unhappy with a financial product or service, you have the means to complain. As with many complaints, you must first give the company the chance to put things right. If this cannot be achieved then there are other routes, such as the Financial Ombudsman Service.

However, before the Ombudsman will take up your complaint you must be able to show that you have followed the company complaint procedure and have still received no satisfactory solution to your problem.

Complaints schemes generally

The Financial Ombudsman Service. This provides a single complaints scheme divided into three specialist divisions for banking and loans, insurance and investments. It covers the following types of companies and organisations:

- Banks
- Building societies
- Financial advisors
- Firms dealing in futures and options/ Friendly Societies
- Fund managers
- Life insurance companies
- Pension providers
- Stockbrokers

The Pensions Advisory Service. PAS provides initial advice and conciliation for complaints about employers pension schemes.

The Pensions Ombudsman. This ombudsman decides on complaints relating to employers pension schemes not resolved by OPAS.

The General Insurance Standards Council. This is a voluntary scheme handling complaints about general insurance brokers such as those selling motor and household cover.

The Property Ombudsman Scheme. This is a voluntary scheme dealing with complaints about estate agents from both buyers and sellers. From 1st October 2008, all estate agents are required to register with some sort of Estate Agents Redress Scheme approved by the Office of Fair Trading..

Protection

If you lose money due to miss selling or misadministration, an ombudsman may be able to ensure that you get financial compensation. However, if fraud is apparent, this may not be possible, or if the company or individual becomes bankrupt.

The Financial Services Compensation Scheme

The maximum amounts of compensation are as follows:

Deposits

£85,000 per person per firm

100% of first £85,000

Investments

£50,00 per person per firm

100% of first £50,000

Home (e.g. Mortgage advisors and arrangements)

£50,000 per person per firm

100% of first £50,000
Insurance

Unlimited

Protects 90% of the claim with no upper limit.

Fraud Compensation Fund run by the Pension Protection Fund
This covers member liabilities of occupational pensions in full.

Offshore compensation
Investors should bear in mind that these schemes do not apply to firms based outside the United Kingdom. Although some offshore investment centres, such as the Isle of Man, may have their own compensation schemes, others do not. When investing outside the UK take great care to gain as much information as possible from the institution concerned.

****

2

Mortgages and Property Finance Generally

Most people purchasing a property will need a mortgage. There are many products on the market and deposits are not always required. However, it is crucial that you are in possession of all the facts when making a decision about a mortgage.

Financial advisers will give you plenty of advice but not always the best advice. Sometimes it is better to go to the lender direct. Before you talk to lenders, work out what your priorities are, such as tax advantage, early repayment and so on. Make sure that you are aware of the costs of life cover.

Lenders-Banks and building societies

There is little or no difference between the mortgages offered by banks and building societies. Because banks borrow against the wholesale money markets, the interest rate they charge to borrowers will fluctuate (unless fixed) as and when their base rate changes. Building societies however, which will rely more heavily on their savers deposits to fund their lending, may adjust the interest rate charged for variable mortgages only once a year. This may be a benefit or disadvantage, depending on whether rates are going up or down.

Centralised lenders

Centralised lenders borrow from the money markets to fund their lending and have no need for the branch network operated by banks and building societies. Centralised lenders, which came to the fore during the 1980s, particularly the house price boom, have been criticised for being quick to implement increases but slow to implement decreases, through rate reductions. This is, simply, because they exist to make profit. Therefore, you should be cautious indeed before embarking on a mortgage with lenders of this kind.

Brokers and "independent" financial advisors

Brokers act as intermediaries between potential borrowers and mortgage providers. If they are "tied" agents they can only advise on the products of one bank, insurance company or building society. If they are independent they should, technically, advise and recommend on every product in the market place.

A word of warning. It is up to you to ask detailed questions about any product a broker offers you. You should ask about fees. If possible, you should arrange a mortgage direct with a bank and avoid so called independent brokers.

How much can you borrow?

There is a standard calculation for working out the maximum mortgage that you will be allowed. For one borrower, three times annual salary, for a joint mortgage, two or two and a half times combined. Lenders, however, will vary and some will lend more. Be very careful not to overstretch yourself. As stated, banks and building societies have tightened up their lending criteria and mortgages are hard to obtain without hefty deposits. At the time of writing, the Financial Conduct Authority have introduced tough new rules to ensure that no one can borrow more than they can afford to repay. These rules represent a further tightening up after the fiasco of the last ten years which has ultimately led to the present crisis. Under the new rules, interest only mortgages will only be offered to people with a firm and clear repayment plan, rather than simply relying on the rise in house prices to cover repayment of the capital. Lenders will also have to take account of future interest rate increases on repayment costs.

Mortgage Market Review

New rules came into force in April 2014 means that those seeking a mortgage should brace themselves for a long wait to see a mortgage adviser, three-hour interviews at the bank and forensic analysis of your daily spending habits.

Even after jumping through all those hoops, success is not guaranteed – experts have warned thousands of buyers and home owners are likely to be rejected because they do not meet the new requirements.

The City regulator, the Financial Conduct Authority (FCA), has introduced the new rules, known as the Mortgage Market Review, to ensure borrowers are issued with mortgages they can afford both now and in the future. The FCA was concerned that lenders were making it too easy to get a mortgage before the financial crisis. Many households borrowed too much money and found they were unable to keep up their repayments when the financial crisis struck.

So-called "self-cert" loans, where borrowers declared their income but did not have to prove or "certify" it, were common and people routinely exaggerated earnings to borrow more. Interest-only loans also caused problems. Borrowers flocked to these deals because their monthly repayments were lower, but they had no way to repay the capital at the end of the loan.

To ensure safer lending in future, mortgage providers are now responsible for assessing whether customers can afford the loan in the long term. This includes buyers and those who are remortgaging and want to increase the size of the loan, vary the time frame or transfer it to a new property.

Deposits
Most banks and building societies used to lend 95% maximum, some more than that. However, for now those days are over, although some high mortgage loans are now reappearing. Lenders will usually require higher deposits. The best source of information for reputable lenders is in the weekend newspapers. However, still, the more that you put down the better deal that you are likely to get from the lender.

Help to buy ISA
We will be discussing ISA's further on in the book, but the Chancellor has introduced a Help to Buy ISA in the 2015 budget, which comes into effect in Autumn 2015. These apply to first time buyers over the age of 16. It will not be possible to hold a Help to Buy ISA and a Cash ISA at the same time. For every £200 saved in this ISA the government will deposit £50. This means that when £12,000 has been saved the government will contribute an extra £3000. This is to be used towards a deposit and can be claimed when buying a property. the bonus will be available on homes costing up to £450,000 in London and £250,000 elsewhere.

Help to Buy Scheme
This is a scheme introduced by the government to help purchasers with the cost of buying a home. The scheme is in its final phases being withdrawn at the end of 2016. To be eligible for help from Help to Buy, you must:

-Have a deposit of at least 5%;
-Be looking to buy a home worth £600,000 or less;
-Be purchasing a property you intend to live in most of the time;
-This means you can't buy a property you intend to let out or use as a second home.

There are two parts to the scheme - equity loans and mortgage guarantees

Help to Buy scheme - mortgage guarantees
Most of the UK's biggest mortgage lenders have signed up to offer Help to Buy mortgages, as well as smaller lenders.
Help to Buy mortgages work like this:

-You'll put down a deposit of at least 5%
-You can borrow up to 95% of the property's price from a mortgage lender.
-The government will then guarantee any mortgage borrowing above 80% of the property's value.

For example, if you took out a 85% mortgage the government would guarantee to repay your lender up to 10% of its value if you defaulted.

But all of this goes on behind the scenes, for you as the borrower it is no different to any other mortgage. You are responsible for repaying the whole loan and could face repossession if you fell into arrears.

For the lender, this will mean that lending to people with small deposits will carry much less risk, so it should create much more choice for borrowers. However the government is giving lenders the freedom to set their own interest rates as part of the scheme, so there are no guarantees you'll get an attractive rate.

How equity loans work
A Help to Buy equity loans are only available to people who want to buy a new build property. They work like this:

The government lends you up to 20% of the property's value as an equity loan;

-You'll need a deposit of at least 5%;
-You'll need to get a mortgage of 75% of the property's value.

So if you wanted to buy a house worth £200,000, it would break down as:

-A £40,000 loan from the government;
-A £10,000 deposit put down by you;
-A £150,000 from a mortgage lender.

The benefit to getting an equity loan from the government is that with a larger amount to put down, you'll hopefully get a better mortgage rate from your lender.

Equity loans - what you'll have to pay back
-The equity loan is interest free for the first five years;
-From the sixth year onwards you will pay an admin fee;
-The admin fee will start at 1.75% of the loan;#
-The admin fee will increase every year by any increase in the Retail Prices Index plus 1%.

Remember, you will be paying these fees in addition to your mortgage repayments and the equity loan from the government will not be decreasing in size (unless you opt to repay part of it early). So, over time the cost of the admin fee could become pretty expensive.

You will need to repay the equity loan in full after 25 years, when your mortgage term finishes or when you sell your home - whichever happens first. You will repay the market value of the loan at the time, rather than a fixed cash amount. In practice, this means:

-You take a 20% equity loan to buy a property worth £200,000, or £40,000;
-When you sell the property, it's worth £250,000;
-You repay £50,000 - this is 20% of the new value of your home, not the amount you borrowed;
-If the property had dropped in value, you'd pay less than you borrowed.

You can also choose to repay part of the loan early in chunks of either 10% or 20% of the total value.

Joint mortgages
If you want a joint mortgage, as for any other shared loan you and your partner have a shared responsibility for ensuring that the necessary repayments are made. If something happens to one partner then the other has total responsibility for the loan.

Main types of mortgage
Endowment
With this type of mortgage, you have to take out an endowment insurance policy which is then used to pay off the mortgage loan in a lump sum at

the end of the term. There are a number of different types designed to achieve the same end:

- Low cost with profits. This is the usual sort of endowment, guaranteeing to pay back part of the loan only. However, because bonuses are likely to be added, it is usually enough to pay off the loan in full;
- Unit linked endowment. With this, the monthly premiums are used to buy units in investment funds. The drawback is that there is no guarantee how much the policy will be worth on maturity, since this depends on how well the investments have performed.

A word of warning. Endowment products were pushed heavily by financial brokers. There was an obsession with them in the 1980's. This is because they earn big commission for those people that sell them. Like a lot of salespeople, motivated by greed salespeople, some advisers failed to reveal the down side. This is:

-Endowments are investment linked and there is no guarantee that they will have matured sufficiently at the end of the term to repay the mortgage. This leaves you in a mess. A repayment mortgage will definitely have paid off the mortgage at the end of the term. If you change your mortgage and decide that you do not wish to continue with an endowment mortgage, and so cash in the policy early you will almost certainly get a poor return unless it is close to maturity. In the early years of the policy, most of your payments will go towards administration and commission (a fact that your broker does not always reveal). The alternative in these circumstances is to maintain the endowment until it matures, treating it as a stand-alone investment which will, hopefully, make you some money eventually.

Repayment mortgages

This mortgage, where the borrower makes regular repayments to pay the mortgage off over the term is a fairly safe bet. However, if you plan to move house every five years then this will not necessarily be the best mortgage for you. With a repayment mortgage, you pay interest every month but only a small proportion of the capital, particularly in the early years of the mortgage. An endowment mortgage, while more risky, could be better for you under these circumstances, since you can transfer the plan from property to property, while it can, hopefully, grow steadily as it matures.

Pension mortgages
Similar to the other products except that the payments go into a personal pension plan with the remainder after paying the mortgage forming the basis of a pension. The same characteristics apply as to the others.

Interest only mortgage
The borrower pays interest only on the loan, and decides how he or she will pay the loan off at the end. The lender will want to know this too, particularly in the light of the new rules being introduced, mentioned above.

Mixed mortgages
A new development is that one or two lenders now allow borrowers to mix a combination of mortgages in one deal, customising the mortgage to suit each individual.

Foreign currency mortgages
Some foreign banks offer short-term mortgages in the foreign currency of that bank. Their lending criteria can be much more relaxed than trying to borrow from a British lender. The advantage of this sort of mortgage depends on currency fluctuations. If the pound is stable or rises, the borrower benefits. If the pound drops, the borrower will have to pay more. These types of home loans should be left to more sophisticated investors as there is the potential to get into trouble unless you have a clear grasp on the implications of such a mortgage.

Cashbacks
You probably saw the adverts offering large sums of cashback if you took a particular product. If you read the small print, unless you took the highest mortgage available with the highest deposit then you would not get anywhere near such a sum. This mortgage was typical of the many mortgages on offer in the pre-credit crunch times. You would be very hard pushed to see such an offer now.

What to do if you feel that you have been given wrong advice
The mortgage lending market is very complicated and many people have suffered at the hands of financial advisors and others who have given incorrect advice. Mortgage regulation has not been very tight. However, the basic framework is as follows:

- Sales of mortgage linked investments like endowments or pensions are regulated by the Financial Conduct Authority. Anyone selling investments must be qualified and registered and must be able to clearly demonstrate that the policy that they have recommended is suitable. All registered individuals and firms are inspected by regulators and can be fined or expelled from the industry if guilty of wrongly selling products.
- By contrast, information on mortgages is currently regulated by the industry only, voluntarily, under a code of mortgage practice sponsored by the Council of Mortgage Lenders. Although most of the big players are signed up to the code there are still some who are not. Check first before taking advice.

How to complain

- Complain first to the company that sold you the product, going through its internal complaints procedure.
- If you are unhappy with the firm's decision, approach the relevant complaints body. For mortgage advisors employed directly by lenders, or complaints about lenders generally, contact the Financial Ombudsman Service on 0800 0234 567 or www.financial-ombudsman.org.uk
- For mortgage lenders which are not building societies or banks but which are signed up to the mortgage code, the Chartered Institute of Arbitrators 020 7421 7455 www.ciarb.org will assist.
- If your complaint is about a mortgage broker, contact the Chartered Institute of Arbitrators which may be able to help if the firm is registered under the code.
- Complaints about endowments, pensions and other investments is handled by the Financial Conduct Authority 0300 500 0597 www.fca..org.uk and are dealt with by the financial ombudsman Service.

The most common complaint is to do with endowments. A lot of people bought products which they came to regret. They are a major source of profit to the provider-and all those in between-but the person left holding the problem is the consumer.

If you believe that you have been given bad advice about anything to do with the insurance or investment side of a product then you should approach the Financial Services Authority.

The Building Society Association or the British Bankers Association have free publications that should help you. In addition, the Consumers

Association, "Which" runs regular articles on mortgages. Remember - always ask questions. Never rush into anything. Always take advice if you are uncertain. Banks and building societies themselves are usually a better source, a safer source than individual advisers.

Borrowing and the internet

Almost all lenders have their own sites and many operate internet only loans with keener rates than those available on the high street. But there are also growing numbers of mortgage broker sites, offering mortgage calculators so that you can work out how much you can afford to borrow and how much the true cost of your loan will be. The following are a selection of independent sites:

www.moneysupermarket.co.uk
This is an online mortgage broker with a choice of over 4000 variable, fixed rate, capped and discounted mortgages as well as more specialist loans for right to buy, buy to let and self build property, also self certification loans.

www.moneynet.co.uk
This is an independent on line mortgage broker, offering mortgages from over 100 lenders. Again, as with all these sites it will provide a clear and comprehensive picture of mortgages available and is easy to use, just follow the instructions.

www.moneyextra.co.uk

An independent financial advisor with access to over 4500 products including all kinds of mortgages for all types of client.

What is stamp duty and who pays it?

Stamp Duty — Stamp Duty Land Tax (SDLT) official jargon — is a tax you pay when you buy a home. The buyer pays stamp duty – not the person selling. Stamp duty applies to both freehold and leasehold purchases over £125,000

2. How much do I have to pay?

Stamp duty used to be charged on the whole property price, so that it went up in big jumps. For example, if you bought a property for £250,000 you would have paid £2500 stamp duty; but if you bought a house costing just £1 more, you would tip into the next stamp duty bracket (what used to be 3%) and pay £7500 – a £5000 jump. This slab structure is gone now and from December 4, 2014 stamp duty is applied like income tax.

Stamp duty is charged according to the scale overleaf.

Purchase price of property	Stamp duty rate
Up to £125,000	Zero
Over £125,000 to £250,000	2%
Over £250,000 to £925,000	5%
Over £925,000 to £1.5 million	10%
Over £1.5 million	12%

So, for example, if the agreed purchase price is £275,000. Under the new rules, stamp duty is calculated as follows:
0% on the first £125,000 = £0
2% on the next £125,000 = £2,500
5% on the final £ 25,000 = £1,250
Total stamp duty payable = £3,750

Solicitors' fees
A solicitor has to be appointed to act on your behalf and also of the relevant lender. All lenders have a panel of acceptable solicitors and you should check to make sure that you are using a firm that is acceptable otherwise you could be expected to pay two sets of fees.

Your solicitor will carry out various checks and searches and will make numerous enquiries with the owner's solicitors about any issues you or the lender may need to have clarified before you commit yourself.

Based on a purchase price of £275,000 the fees payable to your solicitor would be approximately: £2000 approx plus vat inclusive of disbursements but excluding stamp duty.

Illustration of Solicitors' Fees and Disbursements
Purchase price £275,000
Legal fees:
Solicitors £400 + vat
Stamp Duty £3,750 (3%)
Local Authority search fee £180 approx.
Land Registry fee £140 approx.
Land Registry search fee £5
Bankruptcy search fee £1 per client

Other searches such as contamination and water and sewerage etc £200

The most important part of the initial cost is, of course, the deposit money. You will normally be expected to provide at least 5% deposit. This money must be from your own savings or a gift from family etc. because if you are borrowing the money it is effectively a 100% loan. The deposit money is paid to your solicitor on exchange of contracts as this is the time of the transaction when you totally commit yourself to the property. You would normally move in two or three weeks after.

Advice for parents helping children on to the property ladder

In spite of the many incentives now on offer to help young people onto the property ladder, prices are still way too high for most people. There are a number of ways for parents to help their children, outlined below.

Help with the deposit

A 'gifted deposit' is one way to help children. Most lenders will want to see a letter from parents confirming no future interest in the property. A gift is also a way to avoid any future inheritance tax liability, assuming that you survive for more than seven years after the money has been gifted.

Saving early

If you have the foresight you should think of saving early for children's deposits through junior ISA's which have an annual limit of £4,080 from April 2015.

There are a number of other ways to help, such as remortgaging your home and also offsetting family savings.

****

3

Life Insurance

The concept of life insurance is by no means a 20th century development. The earliest forms can be traced back to Greek and Roman times. Clubs would be formed and, for a regular contribution, a lump sum would be paid in the event of death of an individual.

In today's society, we are expected to insure for virtually everything and anything and at the end of the month there are normally limited funds to insure for the most important issue, YOU.

Do you need it?

Many people feel they do not need life insurance. In some cases this is true but the vast majority have families and feel that they need to be protected in the event of an unexpected death. It is not always the main income provider who needs all the life cover. Provisions must be made if there are children and the non-working parent spends his or her time looking after them. The cost of employing a child minder or even giving up your full time job must be considered. This could be easily remedied with a basic life insurance policy.

If you have a mortgage the banks and building societies normally insist that you have the relevant life insurance to cover the mortgage debt and in the case of endowment mortgages the life insurance forms part of your endowment premiums, but with repayment mortgages the cost of premiums is extra.

As you are probably aware, if you haven't got any life cover other than in conjunction with your mortgage then you are likely to be under-insured.

If you are in an occupational pension scheme you are likely to have cover as part of your benefits. This would normally work out to be 3 times your basic salary and if you have a personal pension plan you can have life cover up to 3 times and you would receive tax relief on your premiums.

To establish how much life cover you require you need to calculate how much income the family needs to survive each year. Take away any state benefits you would be or are entitled to and then multiply this figure by the number of years your youngest child has before he or she leaves school.

Example

A family requires £15,000 per year income.
No benefits available.
The youngest child is 9. Therefore there is a minimum of 7 years before the child could leave school and start work.
7 x 15 = £105,000 life cover

You could say that the life cover quoted would be too much after the first year, but the youngest child could always go on to sixth form or college and may not actually start work until he or she is 20 years old.

Different types of life insurance

Most forms of life insurance are paid on a monthly or yearly premium basis. The premium you pay will purchase a level of cover and it can be on a fixed or variable term. There are a multitude of insurance policies geared to the individual's needs and requirements, and we will now look at the differences.

Decreasing Term Assurance

This policy is commonly known as mortgage protection and is normally used in conjunction with a repayment mortgage. As we have already discovered with a repayment mortgage the debt reduces further throughout the term and the same can be said about the decreasing term insurance. The amount of life cover will decrease in line with the mortgage. This policy can be written in joint names and is the cheapest form of life assurance available. There is no investment value to this contract and in the event of a claim, the benefits are payable to the estate.

Example

Mortgage Protection Assurance

Male non-smoker age at entry not exceeding 30
Female non-smoker age at entry not exceeding 30

Benefits
Initial sum assured   £50,000
Plan Term   25 years

Monthly cost
Premium payable for 25 years
or until first death if earlier   £9.57
Warning - the contract has no cash-in value at any time.

Level term insurance
This policy works on the same basis as the above, but the life cover will not reduce as the term goes on. For this reason, the premiums are slightly more expensive.

Family income benefit policy
This policy will simply provide an annual income for your dependents instead of a lump sum. This is a good way too ensure that the provisions that you have made are not used up in one spending spree.

Once again, this contract can be written in joint names, but has no investment value.

Whole life
This type of policy is considered to be the most flexible contract in the life insurance market. Unlike the other contracts this policy does have investment value and it is not written on a fixed term. The amount of cover you require can be altered at any time to suit changes in your personal circumstances. The premiums you pay are not fixed and are reviewed every 5-10 years to establish whether the insurance cover can still offer you the level of cover for the premium you are paying.

This policy is quite expensive in comparison to term policies. It is, however a great deal more flexible and it can be written in joint names.

Example
Whole of Life min/max cover basis
Male, non-smoker, age 30 next birthday

Female, non-smoker, age 30 next birthday

Amount of Life Cover payable on first death:

minimum   £10,350

maximum   £114,900

Monthly premium   £25

Critical illness
A new innovation in the insurance industry is the introduction of critical illness insurance.

Surveys have shown that more people are concerned about being diagnosed as having a critical illness than they are of dying. The implications of having a major illness are immense as you could find yourself stuck with the financial commitments but without the income and ability to pay them. The introduction of critical illness means that if you are diagnosed with any of the defined illnesses in the contract, you will receive a lump sum. The amount of the lump sum depends on your premiums and your age. The benefit of critical illness means that you can afford private medical treatment or afford to pay off your debts. Below are listed the main conditions that are considered to be critical illness:

-multiple Sclerosis--heart attack--kidney failure--loss of a limb
-stroke--major organ transplant—cancer—Coma--benign brain tumour
-severe burns

This is not a technical guide or a total list of definitions. It is simply a selection of some definitions. Critical illness can be taken out by itself, or as part of a whole life or endowment. Critical illness does not have investment value. It can be written in joint names.

Example
Male, non-smoker, age next 30 next birthday
Female, non-smoker, age 30 next birthday
Initial monthly premium £25.00
Initial sum assured   £65,000
Life Assured basis   joint life, first event
Cover type   Maximum

The premium is payable until the earlier of the:
- death of the last to die of the lives assured.
- diagnosis of one of the lives assured suffering a critical illness.

The premium will increase annually by the amount required to support the increase in benefits as a result of the Automatic Increase Option.

What the benefits might be
The greater of the sum assured and the encashment value of the plan will be payable on the diagnosis of one of the lives assured suffering a critical illness.

****

4

Savings and Different Savings Vehicles

The fact that interest rates have gone down drastically at the time of writing means that people are now having to look very carefully at where they save their money in order to get the highest return.

People save for a number of different reasons, dependent on their circumstances and on age. Some people save in order to have enough to help their children and others save for a prosperous old age. Whatever the reason, it is important to understand the best vehicles for savings

Those skilled in the art of financial planning consider that a sum of between three and six months expenditure constitutes an adequate fund for emergencies. This will depend on your employment status as if you are self-employed then you may need more due to the fact that you will not get sick pay unless you are insured.

This emergency cash should be placed in an account that is readily accessible, probably in an instant access account which allows you to withdraw without penalty. However, these accounts traditionally pay the lowest form of interest and it is advisable to shop around.

There are a number of newer accounts, such as telephone only accounts which offer a higher rate of interest with instant access. You are provided with a card so that you can gain access to your money as and when you need it. If the account is joint then both partners should be provided with a card. In addition to phone accounts there are internet accounts. Although some of the providers are large established institutions, some are smaller companies with far less capital. You should always think before investing with any company. Think about your needs and requirements and the security of your capital.

Cash returns

A lot of savers like to have more cash on deposit than they need for emergencies. If you do not need access to the money for emergencies then it is better to put your money in a higher rate account, one which generally needs notice of withdrawal. The longer the period of notice the more interest that you will get on your money.

Postal accounts also pay higher than standard rates of interest and these are useful for those savers who do not require access to their savings over a foreseeable period.

You can get an idea of interest rates by perusing the pages of the dailies and weekend editions of papers, which compare the costs of borrowing and returns on savings. In the United Kingdom rates for deposits are usually quoted gross of tax. Rates may be quotes on two different bases.

The nominal rate is the rate of interest applied to the account, while the annual effective rate (AER) is the rate taking into account the frequency of interest payments.

The nominal rate is not affected by whether you draw your interest or leave it in the account. But if interest is paid more than once a year and you leave it there, you will earn interest in interest and end the year with more in your account.

If you plan to spend all your interest, you can compare different accounts on the basis of their nominal interest rates. If you plan to leave the interest to accumulate, as the table shows, an account with a lower nominal interest rate could give you a better deal if it is credited more frequently. In this case, you should use the annual effective rate as a comparison.

Tax on interest earned

Tax is usually deducted at source in interest paid. This is a requirement of the effective legislation. Tax is deducted at 20%. If you pay a lesser rate of tax then you can reclaim overpaid tax. To have interest on savings paid without deduction of tax, the account holder has to sign a form R85 declaring that you are a non-taxpayer. Parents can sign this on behalf of children. If the interest paid to a child from money given to it by parents is over £10 then this will be taxed as if this were the parent's income.

Banks based outside the UK, i.e. offshore are not subject to UK tax legislation and many of these institutions offer interest gross. Whether you receive it gross or not you are still obliged by law to declare it on your tax return. It is the savers responsibility to declare the tax.

Some National Savings accounts pay interest gross and this is subject to the same rules, i.e. the taxpayer declaring the interest received.

In the 2015 budget, the Chancellor announced that from April 2016, the first £1,000 of interest from savings will be tax free. It will be interesting to see how attractive low interest ISA's will be after this date.

The choice of accounts

There are a wide variety of accounts available from banks and building societies. Many accounts have differing features. Most pay variable interest but some pay fixed rates. The following are some of the accounts on offer.

Children's accounts

These accounts sometimes offer better variable rates than can be gained on a small deposit on a regular savings account. These accounts can also offer free gifts for children, such as magazines, moneyboxes etc.

Instant access accounts

These permit withdrawal of capital without notice, though there is usually a restriction on how much cash can be withdrawn on one day. The interest rate is variable. Interest may be credited yearly, half yearly, quarterly, monthly or daily. With most accounts, the rate will depend on the amount invested.

Internet accounts

These accounts can only be set up over the internet. The initial transfer is made from your current account, as are future transfers. Interest rates are usually higher than traditional accounts.

ISA's

The individual savings accounts can contain cash, equities (stocks and shares) or insurance.

You can take out an ISA each year. You can invest up to £15000 per year in an ISA (2014-15) and £15,240 from 2015/2016. You can invest all in a cash ISA or split it between cash and investment ISA's. From Autumn 2015, a help to Buy ISA will be launched which is designed to assist first time buyers with deposits for housing. For every £200 paid in the government will contribute £50 extra, so for every £12,000 saved the government will contribute £3000.

Children's ISA's have a savings limit of £4080 from April 2015 and can provide good vehicles to build up a lump sum for the futire.

Monthly income accounts

These types of accounts may have a minimum notice period for withdrawal. The income is usually paid direct to your current account and there is usually a £250 minimum amount.

Notice accounts

Money can be withdrawn without penalty by giving the appropriate amount of notice. If you withdraw without notice you will lose interest on the amount you would have been paid during the notice period. There is usually a minimum deposit of £1000 or more.

Postal accounts
Some building societies offer these accounts, where deposits and withdrawals can only be made by post. Interest rates are variable and may be higher than on instant access accounts, as are the minimum investments required.

Telephone accounts
The initial deposit is made by cheque. You set up a direct debit arrangement on your current account and can then transfer money between it and your telephone account. You have to set up a security code and cite this when calling to transact business. Interest rates are usually very competitive.

Time deposits
The interest rate is fixed for the time of the deposit, often 30 days onwards. There will be a penalty for early withdrawal. Interest is usually added at the end of the period that is fixed and is usually gross of tax.

Fixed-rate investments
You can commit your money for a fixed period; say five years, at a certain rate of interest, say 3%. If rates are at 0.5% this may seem attractive but rates can rise during the period. Before investing for the longer term at fixed rates you should consider carefully the market in the longer term and decide whether you want to make this gamble. Fixed interest rates will offer you a reasonable return over the period and it is difficult to predict interest rates over the longer term.

Short-term fixed-rate investments-Escalator bonds
These are issued by building societies and pay a rate of interest that rises each year for a fixed period. Since these are fixed rate accounts you cannot get it back early or there can be a significant financial penalty. You should always think about the consequences of your wish to invest in this type of product.

Fixed rate bonds
These accounts pay a flat fixed rate of interest for a fixed period from one to five years. Early withdrawal is not usually permitted without a penalty. There will be a minimum investment.

Guaranteed growth bonds

Issued by insurance companies, these guarantee a fixed rate for a specified period, usually between two and five years. A lump sum is paid at the end of the term. The return is treated as having borne basic rate tax so there will only be an additional liability if you are a higher rate taxpayer.

Guaranteed income bonds

These pay a fixed income for a specified term, usually two to five years. The tax treatment is the same as for the above bonds.

National Savings Certificates

These grow in value at a fixed rate for a period of up to five years. The profits are exempt from tax and there are limits on how much you can invest.

National Savings Pensioners Guaranteed Bonds

These pay a fixed amount of income over two to five years. The interest is taxable but is paid without deduction at source.

Unit trust savings plans

Unit trusts and open-ended investment companies are similar in having a pool of money which they manage on behalf of individual and corporate investors. The pool expands or contracts depending on the additions or withdrawals into it and the value of a unit or share is the value of the investments in the pool divided by the number of units or shares in issue. A wide variety of funds are available, investing in a variety of areas and countries. Minimum monthly savings are from £30-£50. The income received is taxable and will usually be taxed at source. Higher rate taxpayers will receive a certificate showing what they have paid at source and they will be personally responsible for any extra payments. Costs vary from 1%-5% of each contribution with an annual charge of 0.5% to 2% of the value of your assets. You can take out a plan in the name of a child.

Investment trusts

Unlike unit trusts or open-ended investment companies, investment trusts do not issue new shares to savers but buy existing shares through the stock market. This is because investment trusts have a fixed pool of assets and the price of a share in the market may be higher or lower than its net asset value. These schemes are run by investment trust managers. They usually subsidise the costs of the plan, which are much lower than the costs of buying investment trust shares through a stockbroker. The annual charges are between 0.5% and 2%. The taxation rules and child rules are the same as for unit trusts.

With profits savings plans

With profits savings plans are in the form of endowment polices issued by insurance companies. Though they are life policies, they provide very little life cover. Most of the premiums that are paid are used to invest in the companies with profits fund, which is a giant pool of assets usually worth billions of pounds. The fund will hold a variety of assets including fixed rate investments, UK and overseas shares and property.

The with-profits policy has a sum assured, which is the minimum amount that is paid on death or at the maturity rate. Two types of bonus are added to the sum assured. Reversionary bonuses are added each year, often at quite a lower rate of 3% or so. At maturity (or death) a terminal bonus is added which can be equal to al the reversionary bonuses paid. Once a reversionary bonus has been added to a policy, it cannot be taken away, but terminal bonus rates are not guaranteed and can be varied at any time. With-profits policies are of two types. Some have one fixed maturity date, while with a 'flexible policy' you can en-cash it at several different dates, usually at five-year intervals. The charges for with profits policies are typically about 12-15% of premiums over the term. The term for these policies is usually quite long, being anything from 10-25 years so careful thought needs to be given to this type of investment. They are only really suitable if you can sustain your savings over this long period.

Friendly society plans

Friendly societies are permitted to run tax-free savings schemes with low minimum and maximum investments. Some are of the with-profit types, while others are unit-linked. The plans have a minimum term of ten years and the high costs can wipe out other benefits so again careful thought has to be given to this type of investment.

The purpose of saving

The purposes of saving, as we have seen, are many and will differ, depending on your circumstances and long-term view. Some of the more usual savings objectives are to provide retirement income, to pay for children's education (see later) to reduce debt such as mortgage and for general purposes, for life's little luxuries. Whatever you choose you should do so carefully, think about the short and long-term advantages and don't take unnecessary risks.

****

5

Single Premium and Lump Sum Investments

If you are able to consider investing a lump sum of money, you must take great care in establishing your requirements for that investment and also your own future plans. For example:

-you may not be worried about getting a significant return as long as it is likely to better the return you would get from your building society account;

-you need the best return possible over the next five years without jeopardizing capital;

-you aren't worried how the money is invested provided you don't receive a tax bill;

Quite clearly, the important issues to remember when investing a lump sum are:

1. the amount of money you can afford to invest;
2. the term of the investment;
3. the risk involved with the investment;
4. tax implications.

As we have already seen in the regular savings chapter, there are numerous ways in which you can invest your money and the same considerations should be made whether you are saving on a regular basis or a lump sum.

The options available
Your choice of investment will obviously depend on your own personal financial circumstances. Below you will find details of the most popular investments currently available.

Higher interest building society accounts
If you are concerned about the risk attached with investing your money, then you cannot do a lot better than your building society. Although some people may consider investing in their building society as unattractive, and

rates now at the time of writing (2015) are at an all time low, you haven't got any worries about how your money is being invested. For lump sums, building societies often offer a wide range of higher rate accounts with a tiered rate of interest, depending on the size of investment. Most higher rate accounts have a notice period which must be given for any withdrawals. This may not apply, however, if the balance of the account remains over £5,000. A large number of higher rate accounts will allow you to take a regular income on a monthly basis. The interest received on these accounts has already been taxed at a composite rate and should you be a high rate tax-payer, you may have a tax liability on the interest. remember, from April 2016, the first £1000 of interest received from savings is tax fee.

National savings
Most national savings are calculated gross and therefore you would have a tax liability if you are a tax payer, therefore reducing the benefit of investing. There are however, a limited number of savings opportunities that deserve a mention.

Ordinary accounts
This is a basic account which will allow you to invest between £10-£10,000. The interest rate increases for amounts in excess of £500.

Index linked Savings certificates
This is a good way of investing your money over a five-year period especially if interest rates are high. The interest you will receive is fixed and tax-free. For more details about this type of investment go to www.nsandi.com.

Investment bonds
Investment bonds are considered a medium to long-term investment and the investment options range from the with profits investments to investments in the property markets and overseas. The risk is always a major factor in any investment and you should be aware exactly where your money is being invested and the relative risk.

All major insurance companies offer investment bonds and they can be used for both capital growth and income if required. The investment fund is taxable and payments are made net of basic rate tax. There is an allowance however, which will allow both basic rate and higher rate taxpayers to withdraw up to 5% of the fund value each year without liability.

The minimum amount that you can invest in a bond is normally £2,000 and you should consider investing it for a minimum of five years. In the case of an emergency, you would be able to gain access to your money but the value will relate to the period of investment, charges and market conditions.

The main points to remember are that you should invest in a bond that suits your attitude to risk. If you are a higher rate taxpayer you may be able to reduce any liability if you can cash in the bond when the income drops to the basic rate bracket.

Guaranteed Capital Investments

This is a relatively new concept in the insurance industry as your investment is directly linked to the performance of the FTSE one hundred. If you read the financial press or watch the main television news you will always see a reference to the FTSE one hundred. It provides a clear indication of how the stock market is behaving as it monitors the share prices of the top 100 companies in the UK.

From day to day the prices of each company's shares can change for any reason and towards the bottom of the index the smaller companies are constantly competing to secure their position within the top 100.

The growth of the FTSE is often compared to that of banks and building societies (see single premium investments) and over a long term period is considered to be a valuable alternative to the standard options. Traditionally, the FTSE has outperformed the returns offered by building society accounts and for that reason most insurance companies will guarantee that on completion of the five year term you will at least receive your original investment, thereby reducing the risk factor.

The minimum investment is usually £6,000 and the fund and benefits are paid net of basic rate tax. Guaranteed capital investments are offered on limited availability and are not able to provide an income. They are, however, a worthwhile consideration when you are building up an investment portfolio.

Unit Trusts

The purpose of the unit trust is to give individuals the opportunity to invest directly in the stock market. There are a multitude of investment opportunities ranging from UK equities to shares in Japan and North America. In order to overcome the charges and realise a profit, you must look at investing your money in a unit trust for at least three years or longer.

Unit trusts can be used for capital growth or income and you should obtain help from a financial advisor to choose the most suitable trust for your performance. Once you have chosen your trust and paid your money, you will be issued with a certificate. It is very important that you keep this in a safe place as you will need to produce it when you cash it in.

To establish how well your investment is doing, you can phone the trust managers or look at the share page of any quality newspaper. You will normally see two columns, the offer price and the bid price. For the purpose of selling you must multiply the bid price by the number of units you hold.

The tax implications

Unless you are a higher rate tax-payer it is unlikely that you will have any tax liability on the income or gain of the investment. If you are a higher rate tax-payer there are various ways of mitigating your liability and you should discuss this with a financial advisor before committing yourself to any investment.

****

6

Protecting Income

This chapter is written in the light of the recent uproar regarding the miss-selling of payment protection insurance. Banks recognized the problem and agreed to pay compensation to victims. Nevertheless, we all realise the importance of life insurance and the main lesson has been to check the policy thoroughly before buying. We do however mainly neglect the need to ensure that there is adequate protection to cover accidents or illness that prevent us from working and therefore maintaining our normal standard of living.

Most employers restrict the length of time that they will make full payment to the employee in the event of illness and the self employed are likely to receive even less.

To protect against accident or sickness, you can take out an income protection plan. For a monthly premium you can cover a pre-determined amount of money relative to a maximum two thirds of your income. The premium you will pay will depend on:

1. How much benefit you require;
2. Your age;
3. How long you are prepared to wait before you receive benefits (deferment period 4 weeks - one year);
4. Your medical condition;
5. Your occupation.

If you make a claim on your income protection policy, the benefits will be paid to you until such time as you are able to return to your normal job or one of a similar nature, or your expected retirement date. This type of cover will not protect you against redundancy.

In the event of a claim, the benefits you receive represent and replace your income and therefore attract tax at the relevant rate.

Cover offered by banks and building societies

The threat of losing your job is common in today's society and it is something that could ruin your lifestyle and bring great hardship to you and your family.

The banks and building societies are of course aware of this and therefore offer you the opportunity to apply for a scheme which will protect you and your partner (in the case of a joint mortgage) against accident or sickness or involuntary redundancy. This is sometimes referred to as mortgage payment protection or payment care.

The premiums for these types of schemes range from £6 per £100 of cover to £9 per £100. A claim can only be made and benefits paid once you have been unable to work for a period of three months, after which stage the benefits are normally paid for a period of one to two years for sickness and also for redundancy. Some insurers when paying benefit will send a cheque direct to your lender each month to ensure you are using the money for the purpose that was intended.

These schemes have proved very popular and you should seek further information about them from the relevant lender, as you are not likely to be given a chance to take out a policy after your mortgage has been completed.

You can also allow for extra benefit from these policies to cover the cost of any endowments or life insurances that may run in conjunction with the mortgage.

This type of cover is of benefit to the employed but the redundancy cover is obviously of no benefit to the self-employed and a good permanent health insurance would be more relevant. If the benefits of the scheme are paid direct to you, that would constitute income and income tax would be payable at the relevant rate.

****

7

Taxation

Income Tax

Regardless of whether we are employed or self-employed, we all have to accept the fact that the Inland Revenue are going to take a percentage of our income in the form of income tax and there is nothing we can do to avoid it.

The employed and self-employed are treated in slightly different ways and therefore we shall look at each individually, once we have assessed the structure of income tax. You should check your current tax allowances with HM Revenue and Customs as they are subject to annual change.

Personal allowance

Most people are allowed to receive a certain amount of income before tax is payable. This is known as the basic personal allowance. In 2015-16 basic personal allowance is £10,600. In 2014-15 it was £10,000. If you earn above £100,000 it is progressively withdrawn, at the rate of £1 for every £2 above £100,000 you earn. This means that if you earn £121,200 or more (2015-16) you receive no personal allowance and all your income is taxed. For 2013-14 this figure was £120,000.

Personal allowances for older people

People born before 6 April 1938 may qualify for a higher amount of tax relief, age-related personal allowance. Depending on their income, this could mean a personal allowance of £10,660 in 2015-16 (the same figure as 2014-15).

You are only entitled to the full amount of higher age-related allowance if your income during the 2015-16 tax year is under 27,700, however (£27,000 for 2014-15).

If your income is above £27,700 you'll lose the higher allowance at the rate of £1 for every £2 that your income exceeds £27,700.

Above £27,280 (2015-16), you lose any higher allowance and get just basic personal allowance.

Income above £100,000

If your income is above £100,000, basic personal allowance is further reduced by £1 for each £2 earned over the £100,000 limit, irrespective of age.

Blind person's allowance

You may also be entitled to an additional allowance if you or your spouse or registered civil partner are blind or have severely impaired sight.

This is another full relief allowance as it is treated in the same way as the personal allowance, so increases the amount of income you can receive before you start to pay tax. In 2015-16 this allowance is £2,290.

In England and Wales

If you live in England or Wales, you will need to be certified as blind and appear on a local authority register of blind people to claim this allowance.

In Scotland and Northern Ireland

If you have not been certified as blind and live in Scotland or Northern Ireland you will qualify for the allowance if your eyesight is so bad that you are unable to perform any work where your eyesight is essential.

Unused balance

If your income is not enough to make use of the allowance, any unused balance can be transferred to your spouse or registered civil partner. Married couples get certain tax breaks

Married couple's allowance

You only qualify for this allowance if you or your husband, wife or registered civil partner were born before 6 April 1935.

Unlike the personal allowance, the married couple's allowance is not an amount you can earn before you start paying tax. Instead, it's a restricted relief allowance, which means the tax you pay is reduced by deducting 10% of the allowance from your final tax bill.

The married couple's allowance for 2015-16 is £8,355. So if you receive the full married couple's allowance of £8,355, £835 will be taken off your tax bill (£8,355 x 10%).

Income above £27,700

The amount of married couple's allowance you receive may be reduced if your income is more than £27,700.

If your income is above this limit, age-related personal allowance is reduced first, by £1 for every £2 'excess income', until it falls to the basic personal allowance of £10,600. If your income is above £100,000 your basic personal allowance is then reduced at the same rate.

After this you lose married couple's allowance at a rate of £1 for each remaining £2 of 'excess income', until you reach minimum married couple's allowance of £3,220 in 2015-16.

Marriage transferable tax allowance

Additionally, from April 2015, married couples born after 1935 will be able to transfer up to £1,100 of unused personal allowance (Marriage transferable tax allowance).

Claiming maintenance relief

You can claim this relief for certain maintenance payments you make if you or your ex-spouse or registered civil partner were born before 6 April 1935 and you pay the maintenance under a legally binding agreement.

It works in a similar way to the married couple's allowance. Your tax bill will be reduced by 10% of the maintenance relief allowance or the amount you pay in maintenance, if that amount is lower.

In 2015-16 the maintenance relief allowance is £3,220, so if you are eligible to claim you'll be able to deduct £322 or 10% of the amount you pay in maintenance, if that's lower.

The Employed

If you are employed your tax affairs are conducted on the fiscal year or financial year which is 6th April to 5th April the following year.

You are taxed on what is known as Schedule E (Pay As You Earn) which means that both tax and national insurance will be deducted by your employer before you receive your salary cheque. You therefore receive your salary net of tax. This is without doubt the simplest way to conduct your tax affairs as there is very little further communication you need to have, if any, with your tax office.

At the end of the financial year you will receive a P60 which is a statement of your full year's earnings and it will contain details of how much tax and national insurance you have paid as well as pension contributions if you are in an occupational pension scheme.

You should always keep your P60 in a safe place as it often requested by banks and building societies for mortgage or loan purposes.

If you work for a large employer you may receive fringe benefits such as a company car, mortgage subsidy, or private medical insurance. These are very worthwhile benefits but you must remember they are also taxable benefits which will mean that your personal allowance will reduce to account for the real value of these benefits. If you have such benefits but notice your tax code hasn't changed then it is your responsibility to inform your tax office, as failure to do so may mean that in future years they could claim payment for undisclosed benefits.

Not all benefits are taxable, however, and the most attractive one is obviously a company pension scheme. In recent years a great deal of companies have moved towards Performance Related Pay and there is a tax concession which will allow them to pay a bonus known as Profit Related Pay up to a maximum of £4000 pa without any tax liability regardless of your marginal rate. This is obviously an excellent concession for everyone concerned. Employees who earn less than £8500 receive lenient treatment with regard to the cost of any benefits they receive.

When you leave employment you will be provided with a P45 which is similar to a P60 but is for the benefit of your new employer to use in order to calculate your earnings to date and therefore make the necessary stoppages in your salary. It is always worthwhile taking a copy of your P45 for your own reference.

The self-employed

If you are self employed your own tax year can be any period of 12 months you want. In the eyes of the Inland Revenue you will be taxed on what is known as Schedule D and pay Class 2 National Insurance contributions.

Being self employed means that the money you receive for the services you provide will be gross and therefore no tax will have been deducted.

It is advisable that you keep an accurate record of all the money you receive and receipts for any money you spend in connection with your business activities. At the beginning of April you would normally receive a tax return form which explores all the potential sources of income you may have. This must be duly signed and returned within a month.

A large percentage of the self employed use the services of an accountant, as they best know the ways in which your tax liability can be reduced and their services certainly make it easier if you are self-employed and are hoping to take out a mortgage.

HM Revenue and Customs will negotiate with you or your accountant once they have details of your year's earnings and business expenses. Once the expenses have been taken from the gross figure this will leave your net income and therefore the amount upon which you will be expected to pay tax.

Your tax liability is normally paid in 2 installments, the first on 1st January and the second on the 1st July. The Inland Revenue, however, do not wait for your accounts to be completed and in most cases you will be expected to make installments based on assessments of your expected income and once your accounts are finalised you will then be informed of any over or under payment.

Capital Gains Tax

If you have successfully bought and sold investments, antiques and property etc., you may find that you would be liable for capital gains tax.

Everyone is allowed to make a profit on opportunities that they fund with their own capital. There is, however, a limit, which you should check with HMRC, and any profit/gain that exceeds that figure would be liable for capital gains tax at the individual's marginal rate.

Inheritance Tax

The subject of death is one which is rarely discussed openly and inheritance tax is thought to be an issue that is largely limited to the wealthy. This however, is a misconception, as inheritance tax will affect more people now than ever before. In order to establish whether you are going to have an inheritance tax bill, you must assess the total value of the estate left by the deceased. This would include all assets and any gifts made within the preceding seven years. If the total figure exceeds £325.000 (2015-16) there will be a liability on the surplus of 40%. If the estate totals less than £325,000 there will be no liability. You should check these limits with HMRC as they are subject to change.

It now becomes clear that if you have been able to build a reasonable amount of savings, paid off your mortgage and may have received a pension lump sum and an inheritance yourself, you could be bordering on the £325,000 limit and your estate would be liable for inheritance tax. You should not restrict your own lifestyle in order to reduce your beneficiaries' tax bill but if you can afford it there are various options and exemptions that could substantially reduce the future liability.

Exemptions

1. There is no inheritance tax between husband and wife.

2. To a U.K charity.

3. Gifts that total £3,000 a year.

4. £250 gifts made to anyone and however many people you like. This cannot be given to the same people as the £3,000.

5. Wedding presents, £5,000 from a parent, £2,500 from a grandparent, £1,000 from friend or family.

6. Part of a divorce settlement.

7. To support female parent-in-law if she is divorced, widowed or separated.

8. Selected agricultural land or business assets and unquoted shares.

Gifts made seven years before death
Any gifts that the deceased made in the last 7 years of his or her life will be liable to inheritance tax on a sliding scale and the value of the gift will also form part of the estate.

In order to reduce the liability you could write any life insurance policies you have under trust and should you die, the benefits of your policies would not form part of your estate, but be payable to your spouse or children, therefore avoiding possible inheritance tax.

For more detailed advice on taxation you should go to the HMRC website at www. hmrc.gov.uk

Changes announced in the 2015 budget
The chancellor announced changes to the income tax regime. the annual self-assessment tax return will be simplified and replaced by digital tax accounts over the next five years. Individuals and businesses will be able to submit their accounts at a time to suit them via their computer tablet or mobile. From April 2015, National Insurance will be abolished for the employment of people over the age of 21. This will include the employment of apprentices from 2016. A review will be commissioned into the avoidance of inheritance tax through deeds of variation. The minimum wage will be increased to £6.70 in the autumn with the aim of boosting it to £8 by 2020. Class 2 NI contributions for the self-employed will be abolished in the lifetime of the next parliament.

****

8

Borrowing and the Costs of Borrowing

Every year, according to statistics, we are borrowing more and more money. Indeed, if we look at the papers we can see that we are a 'nation in debt'. However, if you can possibly avoid credit, it is much better to do so. When you buy goods on credit or you borrow money you are, in most cases, taking out a high interest loan. It is the aim of banks to sell money for the highest rate possible in order to make profits. The best bet, at the end of the day, is the consumer. Better than the stock market or any other investment.

Obviously, in some cases you will need to borrow money. The main point is that if you do have to borrow get the best deal possible. Read the small print. It is really surprising how few people shop around for a good deal and end up paying over the odds.

Caution before you borrow

One question that you need to ask yourself before you borrow is: do I really need to borrow? Many people are tempted to borrow money even when they have money saved. This is mainly because it is a nice feeling having money in the bank. However, this is an illusion. The interest you pay on your borrowings will always be more than the savings. To borrow when you have enough in the bank to pay for an item is false economy.

If you do not have savings, you should think very carefully about whether you really need to spend the money now or whether you can wait. If borrowing is absolutely necessary it is important to know what repayments you can afford. The quicker you can clear a loan the less you will pay. Once you have run up credit, make repaying it a priority.

Comparisons of costs

It is a fact that any lender will be happy to give you credit, providing that you are seen as creditworthy. If you are in the process of getting a loan make sure that you have shopped around, including using the Internet. To find the cheapest credit you will need to compare different lenders interest rates in the form of their APR (Annual Percentage Rate). The APR is designed to show the true cost of borrowing, and all lenders must calculate it the same way. Arrangement fees and any other charges must be included in the calculation as well as interests. How and when payments are made is also taken into account. This allows you to make direct comparisons between different forms of borrowing, so check that you are being quoted the APR and not the monthly rate of interest which sounds a lot less but is usually more.

Generally, the lower the APR. the lower the cost of credit, but make sure that the deals that you compare are for the same repayment period. The APR, as the name implies, is the cost of credit over one year at a time. If you spread the repayment of a loan over two years the cost will be more than one year even if the APR is lower.

The APR may not be the only factor to take into account when comparing loans. Some lenders will reduce the APR if you take out protection insurance, usually making the overall package more expensive. You should also consider whether rates are fixed or variable. Fixed rates protect you from rate rises and enable you to budget but your payments won't fall either. If rates are reduced your payments are fixed and will not reduce. This is very much a calculation that you have to make. In today's low interest rate climate it may be that any further reduction may be so negligible as not to affect your judgment.

Payment protection insurance

Payment protection insurance is usually offered with credit nowadays. However, bearing in mind the recent huge problems with PPI, and the agreement by the banks to compensate those policyholders who were miss-sold insurance, this again is down to your own judgment. Without a doubt this insurance is useful if you are unemployed or have an accident and cannot pay the loans. CHECK THE POLICY.

Borrowing to pay off other loans

We are bombarded with moneylenders, or their agents (companies set up to sell money on behalf of others) who tell us how prudent it is to put all your eggs in one basket. This normally involves re-mortgaging. You should try to restrict yourself to conventional lenders. In many cases, it will appear cheaper in the short-term to borrow money over a long period. You will save on the monthly outgoings but pay a lot more over the period of the loan. If you need to go down this route you will probably find that re-mortgaging with a bank or building society will be a lot cheaper than a secured loan.

Overdrafts

If you want to borrow for a short period an authorised overdraft will be a good option, providing that your bank offers competitive terms. Some banks charge arrangement fees for borrowing others will apply relatively high rates. Many will have a combination of both. If you overdraw without permission, which the banks favour, the interest rates charged will double. The advantages of overdrafts are that they are flexible but the amounts that you can borrow are limited.

Credit cards

Credit cards are one of the easiest and most popular ways of borrowing money. They are convenient and flexible and there is no need to approach the lender other than in the first instance when applying for a card. Maximum limits vary depending on your own circumstances, but can be between £1000 and £15000 usually. The balance that you run up on your card can be paid as quickly or slowly as you wish subject to a monthly limit, usually 3% or £5 whichever is the lower.

If you clear your monthly balance in full there will be no interest charge. This means that you can gain up to 59 days interest free credit between the time that the transaction took place and the time that it takes you to pay the bill. If you do not pay the balance in full then interest is charged.

Interest rates on credit cards vary greatly. They can range between 5-20% and more, depending on the deal on offer. Many card companies try to attract customers by offering reduced rates on balance transfers. Some give these low introductory rates on new purchases as well. The introductory rate usually lasts six months. This can be useful if you want to spread the payments over a few months but contain the interest payment.

Buying goods and services by credit card can make sense in other ways. If you use your card to buy something worth between £100 and £30,000 you will normally qualify for extra protection under section 75 of the Consumer Credit Act, which makes the card issuer jointly liable with the supplier if there is a problem with the goods. Other perks can also be offered by the card supplier such as free travel insurance.

Personal loans

Personal loans are offered by many organisations nowadays, with the large supermarkets and insurance companies getting in on the act. These lenders can usually offer competitive rates. So can lenders over the internet. If you want to make a major purchase the vendor will usually offer to arrange a loan but it may be more competitive to seek a personal loan elsewhere.

Personal loans are a useful way of borrowing over the medium term if you cannot get an overdraft to cover the period. Between £5000 and £25000 can normally be obtained over periods of 1-25 years. The more you borrow the lower the APR. You should always carefully scrutinise the rates on offer and don't be misled. If you need a borrowing facility that you can re-use, rather than a one-off sum, some lenders offer flexible loans where you agree a monthly payment and are allowed to borrow a maximum multiple of that amount at any time.

Payday loans

Consumers unable to access credit through traditional banking means are increasingly turning to alternative sources, including payday loan companies. Payday, or paycheque loans, are short-term loans that you get in return for your pay cheque or proof of your income. They are basically cash advances on the salary you are expecting and are available online and on the high street.

They can be a way of getting your hands on your wages quicker than you otherwise would, but it is important to be aware of the high interest rates charged and the consequences of falling behind with your repayment.

This type of borrowing is not suitable for those looking to repay their loans over a long period, as they are designed to be short-term loans to deal with short-term personal cash flow issues. If loans are rolled over, debts could escalate and consumers could get into difficulties. They should only be considered if consumers are confident that they'll be able to repay the debt in full when it is due.

If you are considering using a payday loan company, you should look into all the available alternatives first:

Speak to your bank manager as you may be able to get an agreed overdraft

Look into Social Fund Loans - these are government-funded, interest-free loans available to those on low incomes (see below).

Changes to payday loan regulation

On 1st April, 2014, the FCA (Financial Conduct Authority) took over regulation of the consumer credit market from the OFT (Office of Fair Trading). One of the first things the FCA did was to crack down on lenders that offer 'High Cost Short Term Credit' (HCSTC), and this includes payday loans. The key changes include limiting the number of times a loan can be rolled over.

Currently if you can't afford to repay your payday loan on time you can usually roll it over to the next month. This flexibility comes as a cost and can quickly lead to a small short term loan turning into a hefty loan term debt.

Usually the balance of your loan is extended by a month, with extra interest and roll over fees whacked on to your borrowing. You generally only have to pay the interest charges upfront when you roll over a loan - but sometimes this can be rolled over as well.

Under the new FCA rules you will only be able to roll over your loan twice before the balance will be due. This protects you from spiralling debts, while still maintaining some flexibility should you need to extend a loan due to exceptional circumstances. Notably the FCA have chosen to go further than the voluntary Good Practice Charter introduced in 2012, which sets a limit of rollovers to 3.

Stopping lenders from trying to collect payment more than twice

Most payday lenders will use a CPA (Continuous Payment Authority) to collect payment. This is a way of taking money from your bank account that gives the lender the right to take payment on any date they like, and any amount they like. This is important because although lenders should let you know when they plan to take payment and how much it'll be, not all do.

CPAs can be a quick and flexible way to pay your bills as they help you avoid default and late payment charges if the lender tries to collect payment from your account and the money isn't there. However, there is growing concern that they are open to misuse, leading to payday lenders taking money from their customers' accounts without warning.

This causes problems if money is taken ahead of other bills, causing defaults on more important debts like your council tax, utilities, mortgage or rent; and leading to bank charges and future credit issues. Under the new FCA rules, lenders will be limited to only two failed CPA attempts. This means that they can't continually try to withdraw money from your account when you don't have the funds available, and instead will need to contact you to find out what's going on.

This limit can be reset if you decide to refinance or roll over your loan and pay the amount you currently owe.

Banning part payments by CPA

As well as introducing a limit on the number of times lenders can try to collect payment via CPA, they'll also be limited to how much they're able to collect.

In addition, caps will be introduced from 2nd january 2015 which will limit the amount of interest that can be charged. They are as follows:

- Initial cap of 0.8% a day in interest charges. Someone who takes out a loan of £100 over 30 days, and pays back on time, will therefore pay no more than £24 in interest
- A cap of £15 on the one-off default fee. Borrowers who fail to pay back on time can be charged a maximum of £15, plus a maximum of 0.8% a day in interest and fees
- Total cost cap of 100%. If a borrower defaults, the interest on the debt will build up, but he or she will never have to pay back more than twice the amount they borrowed.

Secured or unsecured loans

Most personal loans are unsecured. This means that if you do not pay the lender can take you to court but does not have the right to seize any property or possessions. With a secured loan assets such as property (usually property) are used, as security and the lender will take a second charge on your property for the value of the loan. This is known as a second charge loan. Nowadays, there is little advantage in taking out a secured loan as you may be able to find a better rate for unsecured loans, unless you have a poor credit rating.

Interest free or low start credit

This type of credit often seems too good to be true. Many people take it up, particularly on cars or furniture. However, nothing is free and you should look carefully at the terms and conditions. You could find that you are signing up to an interest-bearing loan, with interest waived only if you pay up in full during an initial period. If you miss the deadline to pay of the balance then hefty interest charges will be incurred.

The main principle is that you should always check very carefully what it is that you are getting into.

Hire purchase

Hire purchase is still one of the most common forms of car finance. There are several important differences between hire purchase and personal loans: first, unlike a loan which can cover the whole cost, a cash deposit is normally required with hire purchase. This can also be the part exchange value of your car. Secondly, you are effectively hiring the goods rather than acquiring ownership. This means that until the final payment is made the goods do not belong to you. If you fail to make payments the gods will be repossessed.

Credit Unions

Credit unions are becoming an increasingly important low cost way of borrowing money, particularly for people who find conventional borrowing difficult to access. Essentially, credit unions are financial co-operatives set up and run by people with some sort of common bond. Members may work together or belong to the same profession or live on the same estate. The main principle is co-operation.

Members who save regularly are able to get cheap loans. Apart from the low cost you don't need an established credit record to borrow, your savings record and ability to pay will be the main factors when applying for a loan. To find out if there is a credit union you can join, or how to set one up, contact the Association of British Credit Unions.

If you are turned down for credit

Lenders cannot refuse credit on factors such as race, gender or other but they can turn down your application if they think that you may not be able to repay your debt. Lenders usually make a decision as to your credit worthiness by a means of 'credit scoring' and/or by contacting a credit reference agency.

Credit scoring

Lenders score you on the basis of answers given on your application form. They take into account factors such as whether you own your home or rent, salary, age and occupation. Only those applicants who score above a certain level are deemed credit worthy.

With credit reference agencies, there are a number of specialist organisations which collect factual information about individuals which they pass onto lenders. Their data comes from the electoral roll, other lenders and the courts. This enables potential lenders to find out whether you have defaulted on any other credit agreements, have any County Court Judgments or are bankrupt. Negative information will stay on record for six years. If you are refused credit on the basis of information gained from an agency the lender will give you the name and address of the agency used. You can then contact the agency, with details of yourself and addresses lived in over the last six years and they will supply information. If you find that the information is incorrect then you can ask for it to be corrected and the agency must send the file to any organisation that has asked for it over the last six months.

9

Paying for Education

With the huge variety of standards in education in different state schools, sometimes parents think that the only option is to educate their children privately at a fee-paying school. Fee-paying schools are used more and more by different socio-economic groups who have built up the fees through a private savings scheme. The number of fee paying schools has grown to a point where nearly 600,000 children are educated there, out of a total of 8.2 million children in receipt of education.

Obviously, fee-paying schools are still going to be the preserve of those who can afford them but this chapter gives an insight into planning for the fees. Fees can vary: at one end of the scale, the cheaper end, it can cost £10,000 per year per child. At the upper end, the Eton's of this world, the fees are much higher. If you are intent on sending your child(ren) to a fee paying school then the only way to do so is to save from the child's early age.

If you are fortunate enough to earn enough to save for the child's education then you will be looking to invest a regular amount or a lump sum into an investment product that will, hopefully, grow at a rate higher than inflation. This could be:

- A savings account or National Savings Certificate (low risk)
- An investment or unit trust (medium to high risk)
- A bond fund (medium to low risk)
- A fixed term annuity (low risk)
- Zero preference shares
-

Zero preference shares are shares from an investment trust that has split itself into two types of shares. One produces capital growth but zero income. And the other just takes the income. The term 'preference shares' means that should the trust go bankrupt these shares get paid before other shares on the creditors list. You would need sound financial advice before purchasing these shares.

Your savings should be invested in as tax efficient a manner as possible, probably ISA or a children's bond. You should also be aware that gifts to a child from someone other than its parents could be tax efficient, as children have their own income tax thresholds so can earn up to that threshold without incurring tax liability.

It is recommended that parents start to invest for their children's school fees as soon as a child arrives as obviously the longer that you save the more money you will have. At pre-school and prep-school, fees are lower than secondary fees and it may be possible for you to pay for them out of income and continue to contribute to a savings scheme.

Many schools offer composition fee schemes, where you start paying to the school before the child gets there. This forward paying entitles you to significant discounts from the school. However, these are only useful if your child attends that particular school. You will not receive interest on the money and will lose out if at the last moment you decide not to send your child to that school.

When advance planning for school fees there are a number of points to consider:

- It can be very disruptive to a Childs education to remove them from a school where they have settled in, so make sure you can afford the fees on an ongoing basis.
- School fees tend to increase faster than the rate of inflation, so make your calculation allowing for an increase of 5% per year.
- You will need to plan for all your children. Make an assumption if you don't know how many you will have.
- Be aware of your own likely income growth.

Bursaries, scholarships and other help

Most independent schools have schemes where help is available to pay fees. They are often small amounts, amounting to several hundred pounds or less. This might make a difference however, if you are having difficulty paying fees. Scholarships are usually for more generous amounts and are awarded to children with talents deemed to be worth developing and supporting. In addition, educational trusts do exist and you might find it useful to make enquiries about these to a local education authority.

If you want more information about investing for school fees and the names of suitable advisors The Independent Schools Council can give you names of suitable firms. They can be found at www.isc.co.uk.

University education

The whole area of university funding has changed in the last 20 years or so and it is now costly to send a child to university. Most parents of children who now go to university received a grant and, other than getting part time work, received their education for free (if they went to university). Now, a contribution to education and maintenance is necessary. The burden of fees and maintenance is now largely met through student loans which only have to be repaid on leaving university. This means that the child will be liable to repay its own loan on leaving university. However, many parents wish to help and again a plan is necessary. The current maximum fee is £9,000 per annum with many universities charging this full amount.

Current costs of university

At current costs it is estimated that around £22,200 will be needed over a three-year period, this is without university vacations and doesn't include fees. This relates to £7,400 per year approximately. Some degrees can last considerably longer. The £7,400 is comprised of the following:

Rent £3000
Food and essentials £1200
Utilities and insurance £450
Travel £500
Books etc £450
Clothing and cleaning £400
Leisure £1400

It must be borne in mind that accommodation off-campus can be more expensive especially in larger cities. In out of control rent environments such as London this needs some careful thought.

Student Loan Company

The government has operated its student loan scheme through the Student Loan Company since 1990. For more information on the loans, the terms of the loans and types of loan plus the interest rates and when and how to pay back you should go to www.slc.co.uk. There are income limits per annum before a student has to pay back the loan and nothing has to be paid back whilst studying.

As we have seen above, the outcome of a university education is that students are saddled with debt. Any help that can be given parentally is obviously a bonus. The ways of saving for university fees are the same as saving for other school fees. However, you need to be in a position where you can do this. If you are on the point of sending a child to university then you should make full enquiries to the university of choice about any extra help available if you are on a low income.

****

10

Paying for Healthcare

Healthcare is one of the most contentious issues in modern day society. It is always in the news and it is used as an ongoing political football. The government tries to provide healthcare 'free at the point of delivery' and to a large extent achieves this aim. However, it is true to say that we are living longer than we used to and we are suffering more diseases and incapacities as a result. This means that the NHS has to treat more people than ever before, and there are greater pressures financially and organizationally.

Private medical care and insurance

In certain cases, it is an advantage to have private medical insurance as you will be able to exercise more choice over where and when you are treated instead of waiting in line with other people to treat what may be a painful condition. The drawback is that private medical care does not come cheap.

It is said that for people under forty, on the whole, private medical care insurance provides poor value for money. It is over the age of forty that insurance starts to provide real benefits. It is estimated that on average people in their twenties and thirties will have in-patient treatment once every ten years. The cost of that treatment averages £2000. The costs of premiums over ten years will be in the region of £5000 so the outcome is that you invest more than you get out. Of course, it may be that a serious condition occurs and that you are achieving value for money. However, it is the over-forties who tend to benefit more. Over forty though, premiums start to rise.

If you decide that you want to get private medical insurance there are certain key decisions that you might want to make. If relevant, you should see whether your employer offers such insurance. This is the cheapest option. If, however, this is not an option you will need to shop around for the best deal. Most insurance companies will offer PMI and it is usually through the larger providers of treatment such as BUPA. When selecting which level of cover is appropriate for you, you will be offered a wide range of options. The three standard areas of cover are:

- In-patient treatment (where you stay in hospital overnight or longer)
- Day-patient treatment (where you require supervised recovery time but do not stay overnight
- Out-patient treatment (where you get treatment at a consulting room or surgery)

Generally, most good policies will cover all eventualities but you may have to pay more for out-patient treatment. Other choices you will have to make are:

- Whether you wish unlimited care or a certain amount of cover each year
- Whether you wish to go to any private hospital of your choice or from a selection offered by the insurance company
- Whether cover is only offered is the NHS cannot provide cover within a given period of time (typically 6-12 weeks)
- The size of excess you are willing to pay
- The opportunity to pay for a certain part of the treatment yourself such as consultation)

When applying for PMI you will be required to make a statement about your current health and any previous conditions you may have had. Failure to disclose such conditions can void your policy.

There is a standard list of conditions that insurers tend not to cover. The Association of British Insurers lists the following:

- Pre-existing conditions
- GP services
- Long term (chronic illness)
- Accident and emergency admissions
- Drug abuse
- HIV/AIDS
- Infertility
- Normal pregnancy
- Cosmetic surgery
- Gender realignment
- Preventive treatment

- Kidney dialysis
- Mobility aids
- Experimental treatment
- Experimental drugs
- Organ transplant
- War risks
- Injuries arising from dangerous hobbies

Regulatory structure

Almost all PMI providers in the UK are members of the Association of British Insurers (ABI) and registered with the General Insurance Standards Council (GISC). You should check that your provider is registered before signing up to any scheme.

Long term care

The issue of long-term care is a relatively new one for the finance industry and is little understood by the general public. The structures of the industry and state provision are complex and there are many firms who fail to attain high standards.

Many of us will need long term care in old age. LTC comes in two forms: home care where individuals are looked after in their own homes; and care homes where people go into residential care.

Home care services range from meals on wheels, home alterations to community nursing and day care and respite centres. Local authorities provide the majority of these, but the NHS is responsible for certain areas. The NHS aid is free but usually only available when it is proved that it can improve the patient's medical condition. The general overall rule is that the majority of money is spent on those people most in need.

LTC insurance

These are 'pre-funded' policies where you purchase the cover through payment of regular premiums or with a one-off lump sum payment. You can start the policy at any age, although some insurers only offer policies to people over 40 or 50.

You will decide at the outset as to whether the policy will cover all your LTC expenses or just up to a specified amount and whether it will be a fixed level of insurance or will increase with inflation. Most policies are straightforward insurance only, but you can apply for an investment policy which will pay a capital sum at the end of the term or when you die should you have not used it in all claims. These policies tend to be more expensive.

These are certain risks with LTC insurance:

- The main risk is that you may never need it and if you die before claiming or you stay healthy then the premiums will have been wasted.
- Other risks are that you are purchasing cover for some years in the future (hopefully). It is quite possible that the level of cover may be insufficient for LTC needs. Your insurance company should review the cover every five years.
- The provision of LTC insurance can affect any means tested benefits the state may provide in the future
- Certain illness and disabilities might not be covered. For example mental illness may not be covered.
- Some policies only pay out for a limited time period but most should pay as long as required. This should be checked out when taking out the policy.

The cost of LTCI will depend on age, sex and state of health when taking out the policy.

Immediate needs policies

The downside, as mentioned, of LTCI is that you may never have to claim. Insurance companies will profit out of you. However, this is the risk with most types of insurance. An alternative to funding an ongoing policy is to take out an immediate needs policy.

Immediate needs policies are usually a variant of impaired life annuities. Life annuities are financial policies where in return for your paying a lump sum now, an insurance company guarantees to pay you a regular income each month for the rest of your life. With impaired life annuities insurers tend to be more generous as your life span is considered to be less than it should be.

There are two usual ways to pay for immediate needs policies: with a cash lump sum, or, popularly these days, with equity release. The benefits should be the same as they are determined by the annuity.

These policies are less risky than pre-funded policies as you only purchase one when you know you need it (they are not available until you have a need). However, they are more expensive as the insurance company is almost certain to have to pay you something, although it doesn't know how long. In most cases, when you have purchased an annuity you do not get money back other than the payments. As a result your estate could lose out after your death. Some policies will offer death benefits which are paid out regardless of when the policyholder dies.

Regulators, advisers and providers

The Financial Conduct Authority regulates LTCI provision. This means that all financial advisors will undergo training on LTC issues.

****

11

Investing in Stocks and Shares

The investor

Individual investors can be defined as people who, after meeting all their expenses from their income have a surplus left which they wish to invest, one way or another. There are many reasons for investing, the main one being to meet future needs. Investors can keep a cash reserve in a building society or bank, they can invest in something that they think will appreciate in value, such as property, or shares which can be resold when needed.

Purchasing assets

Assets come in many shapes and forms, cash, premium bonds, securities such as shares in a company or gilt-edged stocks (which are government issued bonds), life assurance policies, works of art, property and so on. Each type of asset has different characteristics which will appeal to different investors. The subject of this book is the stock market and therefore we will be discussing stocks and shares as a viable investment.

The first characteristic of an investment that needs to be considered is an annual return: does ownership of a particular commodity entitle the investor to receive any income and if that is the case, what is the level of that income?

Income can be realised in a number of ways. There is the good old fashioned deposit in a bank or building society, which will give a monthly quarterly or annual return but not at rates that will excite the adventurous investor. Gilt-edged bonds pay interest each year, again guaranteed but relatively low. Investment property will produce a rental income and will appreciate in value (in the good times) and the purchase of shares should, in the ideal world, produce a dividend and possibly capital growth, depending on the share. Again, like everything, the more solid the investment, as we shall see, such as in companies characterised as 'Blue Chip' companies, will generally produce stable but lower returns.

An investor will usually consider the return on an asset as an annual percentage of its value. This is the rate of return, or the yield. The rate of return on a share is known as the dividend yield and is calculated in a similar way to interest from a bank or building society: the dividend paid by a company is divided by the price of the share as quoted on the stock market. Dividend payments on shares are not guaranteed. Companies, for a variety of reasons, can decide not to pay a dividend. However, the other rate of return on shares, capital appreciation, is an equally important consideration to an investor.

Capital appreciation is the increase in value of any money invested. If inflation is higher than the rate of return then money will lose value. Shares are similar to other investments in this respect. They can fall in price as well as rise. Essentially, the total return on any asset comprises income received and the increase in value of that asset (capital growth).

Investors will need to look at the possibility of loss on assets. Different assets have different degrees of risk, usually relating to their potential for appreciation or depreciation. Deposits in banks will rarely if ever depreciate as periodic interest will be added and the investment will be protected apart from a possible loss of value due to inflation.

Ordinary shares carry risks of both falling prices and falling returns. A company's declining profits can result in a fall in the share price and also lead to a company deciding not to pay dividends. Many investors will usually try to create a portfolio of shares, ranging from more high-risk equities to safer homes, so that a fall in the value of one is offset by the growth in value of another.

Basically, different assets have different degrees of return. The main principle is that the higher the return the higher the risk.

Investors will also take into account the degree of ease with which they can convert their asset into cash if need arises. This is known as the liquidity of an asset. The liquidity of an asset will affect the return received. The more liquid an asset, as a general principle, the lower the return. Asset liquidity and asset values are also affected by time. For example, the longer that money is tied up in a bank account the more illiquid that it is. Because of uncertainty about the future, money today is worth more than money tomorrow. To bring their values into balance, and to encourage saving and investing rather than spending, the longer that money is unavailable in the present, the greater the reward.

Hedging and speculation

When weighing up which assets to buy or to hold, an investor will keep coming back to the main consideration: risk. The more risk-averse investor will want as much protection of their assets value as possible. There are various means of achieving this. One basic strategy is called hedging, and it is a version of the strategy of portfolio diversification: the investor will hold two or more assets whose risk/return characteristics to some degree offset each other. One typical example is to hold one safe but low return asset for one high-risk one. A more precise way to hedge is to use derivatives, the range of securities whose price depends on or derives from the price of an underlying security. We will be discussing derivatives later in the book. A put-option, for example, gives its owner the right, but not the obligation, to sell a share at a fixed price (the striking price) on or at a certain date. Owning a put option with the share itself means that the investor's potential capital loss is limited to the loss implied should the share fall to the striking price. If it falls further the investor can use the option and sell at the striking price.

The speculator

On the other side of the hedgers trading is the speculator. This is someone who is prepared to take on the extra risk that the hedger wants to avoid. Speculators are in the market with the intention of making as much money as possible. They believe that they know the future prospects for asset prices better than the majority of investors, and hence are prepared to take bigger risks.

Investors, whether hedgers or speculators, who expect a rise in a particular asset price or in the market as a whole are known as bulls, whilst those who express pessimism about the future of the markets are known as bears.

Markets

Assets are bought and sold in markets. Markets are institutions that allow buyers and sellers to trade assets with one another through the discovery of prices with which both are satisfied. Some traders may meet in physical places. However, in the age of technology this is not necessary. Wherever and however the trading is carried out, what is actually happening is a form of auction. For example a trader may have 100 lots of assets to sell. If there are more or less traders at the suggested price (more or less than 100) the trader will lower or raise the price accordingly. This becomes the current market price.

Financial markets can be classified in different ways. One basic distinction is between primary and secondary markets. In primary markets, new money flows from lenders to borrowers as companies and governments seek new funds. In secondary markets investors buy and sell existing assets among themselves. The existence of the secondary market is generally considered to be essential for a good primary market. The more liquid the secondary market, the easier it should be to raise capital in the primary market by persuading investors to take on new assets. The secondary market allows them to sell should they decide that it is an asset that they don't want to hold.

Markets may also be classified by whether or not they are organised, whether they are regulated by an institution. For example, the London Stock Exchange is an organised market while the over-the-counter derivatives market is not.

Markets can be classified by the nature of the assets traded on them: stocks, bonds, derivatives, currencies, commodities and so on. All of these are distinct markets and there are strong connections between them. These connections grow stronger as increasing globalisation and improved technology allows better flows of information. An investor will need this diverse but interlinked information to allow them to compare and contrast different investments.

****

12

The Stock Market and How it Works-Share Trading

Having looked at the general operations of companies which trade on the stock market, we can now turn to the actual stock market itself.

What is a stock market?
Most people know a market, in the broadest sense, as a number of stalls, trading outdoors, from which you can buy almost any commodity. You can buy fruit and vegetables, clothing, travel goods and so on at an outdoor market. There will be the usual smattering of Del boys and Arthur Daly's. A stock market has the same features, buyers and sellers, an agreed price (with the same smattering of sharp characters). However in stock markets you will usually also have a middleman, essential to guide the investor through the maze of dealings on offer, known as a stockbroker. More about brokers later.

There are many recordings of the first known stock markets in European Cities. In Britain, the first recorded joint stock company was founded in 1553 to finance an expedition to the orient, via a northeast passage. Two of the ships sheltered from storms in Scandinavia and all the crew froze to death. The third reached Archangel and then went overland to Moscow-which was as near to the Orient as they got, and agreed a trading link with The Czar Ivan the Terrible.

There have been many similar ventures. Alongside these ventures London's financial institutions grew. The London Stock Exchange grew out of a small coffee house-the New Jonathans Coffee rooms. As the business grew they moved and eventually in 1801 acquired the name the London Stock Exchange. There used to be a number of stock exchanges dotted around the country but they were eventually amalgamated into one exchange in Old Broad Street London, next to the Bank of England. The stock exchange has since moved as it has had to increase its space as time has moved on and technology and the world markets have grown more complex.

There are two elements to the London Stock Exchange, the first being the official list, which is the main market of the major companies. This is further divided up into groupings by trade. There is a section for distribution, banks, breweries plus one for Techmark (or techMark as it is known) for high-tech companies. In addition there is the Alternative Investment Market (AIM) which is for young companies that do not have the trading record demanded for a full listing. See below for more information.

Stock markets now are remote from companies and deal electronically. London's main market operates on a computerised system called the Stock Exchange Electronic Trading System (SETS) for large shares, with a modified version for mid-market companies. SETS is an order matching system that pairs off the instructions sent to the machine by buyers and sellers. Some stocks are traded using a system called SEAQ (Stock Exchange Automated Quotation System), which is based on an American system. The completed deal is passed to another computer to organize settlement.

The Crest system is trying to eliminate the mass of paper by replacing share certificates with an electronic record. Share certificates are still available for those who want them.

Other UK markets-The Alternative Investment Market (AIM)

AIM is usually known by its initials and is a division of the stock market reserved for small businesses. The idea is that the smaller business will grow and mature and graduate to a full listing. The costs of listing on AIM are almost as high as a full listing. However, the hurdles for acceptance on the AIM are lower. There are about 750 companies from a variety of countries listed and the number is growing.

For the smaller investor in Britain there is an added attraction in that Aim listed companies are regarded by Her Majesty's Revenue and Customs as unquoted, thus providing access to differing tax relief schemes, including business taper and gift relief for capital gains tax, suitability for the Enterprise Investment Scheme, relief for losses and business property relief for inheritance tax (see section on tax further on in the book). The downside, and there always is one, is that smaller companies are less secure and more vulnerable to financial problems

TechMark

TechMARK and techMARK mediscience are specially developed segments of the London Stock Exchange's Main Market, designed for companies at the forefront of innovative technology.

TechMARK was launched in November 1999 by the Exchange to create new opportunities for companies whose business is dependent on technological innovation, and for investors in those companies. Two years later, techMARK mediscience was then launched to focus on companies whose business is dependent on innovation in the development or manufacture of pharmaceuticals, or products or services that are wholly or substantially dedicated to the healthcare industry.

TechMARK brings together companies whose business models require a particularly high level of innovation and investment into research and development programmes. By providing a spotlight on this segment of the Main Market, it helps techMARK companies to build successful relationships with investors – vital to innovation and funding discovery.

And for scientific-research based companies, the Listing Rules take into account business specialisation and facilitate admission to the Main Market.

Who can join?

TechMARK is open to all innovative companies, regardless of size, sector or commercial or industrial activity, country of origin or currency of share trading. There is a broad range of companies operating in numerous sectors on techMARK, from software and computer services to oil and gas and even transport.

TechMARK mediscience companies operate within the techMARK family. TechMARK mediscience specifically includes healthcare sectors such as medical equipment, medical supplies, biotechnology and pharmaceuticals. All techMARK companies share one key attribute – commitment to innovation, research and development.

Ofex

Ofex is the UK's independent public market, dedicated to smaller companies, and based on a quote-driven trading platform. Owned and operated by PLUS Markets Group plc, it is authorised and regulated by the Financial Services Authority. The Market Abuse regime covers all securities traded on the Ofex market.

Since launch, Ofex has served over 500 companies and has not only provided a market for those companies' shares, but also an opportunity to raise equity-based finance. It is a flexible market, with broad appeal to companies, their professional investors, and those investors wishing to invest in smaller companies.

Its robust regulatory framework strikes a careful balance between flexibility for smaller company management teams and the protection required by equity capital investors. A competing market-maker system supports buying and selling shares in Ofex companies, offering liquidity and independent valuation. Investors in UK-based Ofex companies enjoy the tax benefits associated with holding investments in unquoted securities.

Information about the Ofex market can be found at www.plusmarketsgroup.com

Virt X

This incorporates a small rival to the London Stock Exchange called Tradepoint, which started as an electronic order book in 1995 and was itself quoted on AIM. In combination with the Swiss Stock Exchange SWX, it created Virt X, with offices in London and Zurich although all trading is carried out from Zurich. In addition to trading in the normal UK quoted stocks, it has set up clearance and registry systems to allow trading in Eurotop, the 300 largest companies in Europe.

General points about trading on the stock markets

What does the existence of these multiple trading markets mean to the small investor? It means two things. It means that you have easier access to trade shares of companies beyond those that are listed and traded on the London Stock Exchange.

A customers order can be routed to any FSA authorised market where the security trades. Each brokerage firm decides where to route the buy and sell orders it handles.

A brokerage firm tries to get the best price for its customer. This means executing an order to buy securities (stocks, bonds, ETF's (exchange traded funds-more later) etc at the lowest price available at the time the order reached the trading market. When a customer places an order to sell, the brokerage firm tries to execute the order at the highest price available.

The basic order types

It is important to understand the meaning of the different types of buy and sell orders used by brokers to get a trade executed in a specific way. Basically, unless you have an idea of what stock brokers are talking about you will find yourself at a disadvantage. A typical small investor will find that five basic order types will serve most of their investment needs:

- A market order
- A limit order
- A marketable limit order
- A stop order

- A stop-limit order

It is important to understand how each order works and the possible result associated with using each. One basic feature of orders must be clearly understood first. When an order ticket is marked it can be marked in one of four ways:

BUY
'BUY' means the investor is acquiring a securities position with the expectation that the price will rise over time. The words ' Buy' and 'Long' are synonyms in the investment market.

SELL LONG
Order tickets are not simply marked 'sell'. Each ticket must specify whether it is an order to 'sell long' or 'sell short'. Sell long means an investor is selling securities that they already own.

SELL SHORT
'Sell short' is more complicated. It means that the investor is selling securities that he or she does not own. In fact, the securities that are being sold short have been borrowed on the investors behalf by the brokerage firm. The investor is expecting the market price of the securities to decline over the short term so they can buy them back at a lower price. The difference between the higher price at which the securities are initially sold short and the lower price at which they are eventually bought back is the profit to the investor. Needless to say, for the small investor this is a route that is better left alone.

BUY TO COVER
'Buy to cover' means the investor is liquidating a short position. In reality, when the brokerage firm gets this order it buys back the securities that were sold short for the investor. Remember, the brokerage firm had borrowed the securities for the customer. Now it returns these to the lender, which is usually another brokerage firm.

The five basic order types-*A market order*
A market order, whether placed with a broker or using an electronic order ticket, contains only the name of the security and the amount in pounds. It does not specify a price or time, as the examples below illustrate:

buy £1,000 of BT

-or-

Sell £1,000 of Vodafone

A market order must be executed immediately at the BBO, best bid price or offer price, available in the market at that time.

Limit Order

When placing a limit order, the investor specifies the price at which he or she wants to buy a specific security. For example:

Sell £1,000 of Shell at 1.39p

-or- Buy £1,000 of Mears Group at 500p

Importantly, when a limit order is placed, it is understood that the order will be executed only at the specified price or better. the investor who wants to sell wants 1.39p or better. Those who want to sell or want to buy want a certain price or lower.

Marketable limit order

This is a variation on the limit order that is used on many of the computerised order-matching systems. Unlike a traditional limit order, which is entered below or above the market, a marketable limit order is entered at the current price level at which a share is trading. In placing this order, a customer is making sure that the order will be executed only at the current price level or better.

If, for example, a share is trading at 660p and you want to buy shares at this price only, you would enter a marketable limit order with a specified price of 660p. Your order would be eligible for immediate execution. The advantage of a marketable limit order is that if the share price unexpectedly moved above 660p, then your order would not be executed. If the share price moved lower then your order would be executed because the lower price is better than the specified price.

Stop order

Like a limit order, an investor must specify a price, called the stop price, when the order is placed. However, with a stop order, when the security's price hits the specified price, the order is transformed into a market order, and is executed at the security's current BBO, whatever that may be. This is the most useful order for investors who want to limit losses and protect profits. The example below illustrates this.

Let's say that you have just bought a company's shares, which are trading at 660p. When you buy these shares you are, of course, concerned that the price might decline suddenly, resulting in a significant loss. To limit your potential loss you place a sell stop order at 640p, below the price at which you bought the stock. It is important to understand that the price that you specify on a sell stop order is only a trigger. If the share price suddenly plummets and hits your 640p price, the order is immediately transformed into a market order. Subsequently, it is executed at whatever the market price might be at the moment, which may be above or below the stop price. In this case, the sell stop order would limit your loss on the position to around 20p. The loss could be greater if the share price is in free fall

Stop limit order

When an investor places a stop limit order, he or she must specify a stop price and a limit price. For example:

Sell £1,000 of Costain at 3.20p stop 3.50 limit

-or- But £1,000 of Mears at 500p 520 limit

On a sell stop limit order, the limit price is the same or lower than the stop price and on a buy stop limit order the limit price will be the same or higher than the stop price.

Although some of the above may sound a little confusing, especially for the first time investor, it is worthwhile knowing the basics of share sale or purchase terminology.

****

13

Unit Trusts

There are benefits connected to the purchase of unit trusts and investment trusts as opposed to individual shares. With trusts you get a spread of investments over a number of companies, cutting the danger of one of the companies going out of business.

Investment trusts

Investment trusts are companies which invest in other companies on behalf of investors. They are termed close-end funds because the number of shares on issue is fixed and does not fluctuate no matter how popular the fund may be. This sort of investment is convenient for small investors who do not have enough money to buy a lot of shares in different companies thereby spreading the risk. An investment trust will have its money spread across a lot of companies so problems with one company will usually be compensated by a boom in another company. Managers of investment trusts are professionals, so, at least in theory, they will do better than the average person. It is true to say that investment companies are as good as their managers so it is wise to pick a company with a good and known track record.

Most investment funds have a lot of money to invest and they will usually invest in blue chip shares, unless specifically set up to invest in a specific type of share.

The cost of the stockbroker is the same as it would be with other dealings and the government stamp duty and the price spread between buying and selling price remains the same.

Although investment trust managers do have a lot of say in the nature and type of investments, investors will also have some say in what goes on by buying the right investment trust shares. There are trusts specializing in the higher risk stock markets such as Budapest, Istanbul and Madrid (called emerging markets); there are some investing in the Pacific Rim and some concentrating in Japan; some go for small companies and some specialize in Europe and the United States and so on. The spread of investments can be very diverse indeed and managers of investment trusts tend to be more adventurous on the whole than managers of unit trusts.

Some trusts are split capital trusts which have a finite life during which one class of share gets all the income, and when it is wound up the other class of share gets the proceeds from selling off the holdings.

Trusts are quoted on the Stock Exchange so the share price can be tracked and also the asset value of the trust can be calculated. The asset value is comprised of the value of the shares that the trust is holding compared with the trusts own share price.

One main reason that many are priced differently than their real value is that major investing institutions avoid trusts. Huge pension funds or insurance companies do not have to buy in to investment expertise as they normally have their own experts. Therefore trusts are used mainly by private investors.

Unit trusts

Unit trusts have the same advantage of spreading risk over a large number of companies and of having the portfolio of shares managed by professionals. However, instead of the units being quoted on the stock market as investment trusts are, investors deal directly with the management company. Therefore the paper issued has no secondary market. The investor cannot sell to anyone other than back to the management company. The market is seen from the manager's viewpoint: it sells units at the offer price and buys them back at the lower 'bid' price, to give it a profit from the spread as well as the management charge. Many unit trust prices are published in quality papers.

These are called 'open-ended' funds, because they are the pooled resources of all investors. If more people want to get into a unit trust it will issue more paper to accommodate them. Unlike the price of investment trust shares, which is set by market demand and can get totally out of line with the market value the price of units is set strictly by the value of shares the trust owns.

Tracker funds

Tracker funds move with the main stock market index-in the U.K that is usually taken to be the FTSE 100. This type of fund is for the less adventurous investor who looks for a virtually risk free return.

Open-ended investment companies

Open Ended Investment companies or OEICs are placed midway between investment trusts and unit trusts. They are incorporated companies and issue shares, like investment companies. Like unit trusts the number of shares on issue depends on how much money investors want to put into the fund. When money is taken out and shares sold back, those shares are cancelled. The companies usually contain a number of shares segmented by specialism. This enables investors to pick the area they prefer and to switch from one fund to another with a minimum of administration and cost.

Advantages of pooled investments

Pooled investments reduce risk and are therefore a safer home for small investors. However, as they are safe they are unlikely to hit the outside chance of a high performer, as individual share speculators might. As stated earlier, there are many different companies and a certain degree of research and knowledge is essential before committing. To be forewarned is to be forearmed. Quality newspapers will have regular league tables of performance. Be careful too with tables that are published showing performance. Obviously, tables can only look backwards to demonstrate past performance and it is the future that matters. Trusts can do very well, but it may be that they have done well in a sector that has expanded and is now contracting.

Management charges for both investment trusts and unit trusts are usually high. One way of avoiding high charges is to opt for a U.S. mutual fund, which is the same as a unit trust and which has lower charges.

There is also the alternative of setting up your own investment vehicle which has become quite popular over the years. Investment clubs, already very popular in the United States are springing up in the U.K. Basically, a group of people together pool cash for investment in the stock market. The usual way is for each member to set aside a regular amount each month and decide where to invest it. This has the advantages of avoiding charges, spreading investments and also the social spin off. Also, the work of researching shares is spread amongst members.

Exchange traded funds

Exchange traded funds are single shares and are traded in the same way but are in effect representative of the whole index, such as the FTSE 100 or the U.S Standard and Poors 500. It is like an investment trust with a holding in every company comprising one of the indices, but there is an unlimited number of shares and the price is directly related to the index. There is a slight deviation from the underlying portfolio price but it is very narrow. That also means they can be used in the same way, including 'selling short' and included in the ISA's. For a small investor it has the comforts of a unit or investment trust plus the reassurance of not outperforming the market. That means you will never do better than an index but will never lose all your money. There is no stamp duty on the dealing because they are Irish registered companies although there is a small management fee charged by the issuers, usually 0.5%.

****

14

The Benefit of Owning Shares

When looking at shares as opposed to other savings investments, it has to be said that the number of ways a person can invest amounts of their hard earned cash is limited.

There are a whole range of savings accounts paying varying rates of interest, ranging from mediocre to high, all dependant on what you want for the future of your savings, i.e. instant access, long term growth and so on.

Property has proved to be a good investment over the years, particularly with the advent of buy-to-let mortgages. An investor can realise an income and also growth in capital value. However, this type of investment is not for everyone, particularly because of the high capital investment at the outset.

Art is another area of investment but again not suitable for everyone as it requires specialist knowledge when purchasing in order to ensure capital growth.

There are a whole range of other collectibles which rely on at least a basic level of knowledge at the outset. Wine is one area and antiques another.

Because most people need access to their capital to fund a whole range of short and longer term projects, such as holidays, education and so on, buying shares usually ranks way down the list as an investment.

Shares are usually a longer-term investment and the risk involved in the investment depends on the timescale of that investment. Rewards can be measured more easily if a longer term has been allowed to elapse.

The stock market provides a fairly good home for investments for those people who are prepared to accept a degree of risk and can wait for the right moment before cashing in and pulling out. Essentially, money invested in the stock market should not be money that you need to realize at short notice or money that will be realized for your old age. The stock market is only for people who have spare cash to invest and can weather the storm if a loss is made. It is not for those who will lay awake at night worrying about losing money on shares.

If you do decide to invest in the stock market, and there are about 12 million people who have done so in the U.K. then don't put everything you have to invest in the market at once. Keep some aside to invest when a really good opportunity arises.

There are two ways to invest in the stock market, long term (suitable for the small investor) and as an active trader.

Long-term investment

It is true to say that in the long term the stock market has produced a better return on investment than any other alternative form of investment. All of the charts produced to indicate growth have demonstrated that over a period of 30, 50 and more years, returns from shares outperform most other investments. Shares in Britain have, since 1918, produced a return of over 12% a year compared with other investments such as government issued gilt edged securities which have produced just over 6%.

This return on shares has been in the face of the periodic cyclical downturns in the economy and in overseas economies. Cash in a deposit account would have produced 5% in the same period. However, cash in a deposit account is safe and as we have seen shares can be a risk.

When considering the long term, questions of future economic stability will always arise. For sure, at different periods economies will fluctuate and losses will occur but in the longer term these tend to even out and share prices rise, as history has demonstrated.

It is up to the investor to decide what they want from an investment. Do you want income or capital growth? These are not absolute alternatives, since companies that do well hand out handsome dividends (usually) and see their share price rise. Unit trusts and investment trusts as we have seen provide good homes for savings and, at the very least will ensure inflationary growth.

Short-term investments

This is another way of investing, but it is for the experts and people who are sufficiently clued up and will devote time to study the markets. This is the short-term active trading which is built on the tactic of taking advantage whenever share prices move sharply enough to make trading beneficial. The active short-term trader will watch the markets very carefully and look for opportunities such as takeovers and mergers where they can buy and sell relatively quickly at a profit.

Short-term investing usually requires more money than longer term investing as the costs of trading can be higher as brokers fees and government taxes have to be paid.

Perks of owning shares

In addition to the usual benefits of owning shares, such as appreciation of capital and dividend income, many companies try to keep shareholders loyal by offering perks, usually in the form of discounts of one form or another. Channel tunnel has travel concessions offered to shareholders, other nationally known companies such as Iceland and Kwik Fit all provide benefits to investors. A number of fund managers will provide a list of companies that provide perks for shareholders.

****

15

Vehicles for Buying Shares and The Costs of Investing

When considering the initial amount to invest in a parcel of shares, it is important to realise that the less you invest the higher the overall cost of shares, because of fees etc, and the more a share has to rise to make a decent return. It is for this reason that most people in an advisory capacity would say that £2,000 is the minimum that should be invested.

For safety the investment should be spread over a number of companies. The old adage 'don't put all of your eggs in one basket' rings very true here. A common portfolio for a small investor should contain at least 12 companies (but not more as the other factor is that the investor should stay in control of his or her investments). The main aim of all investing is to get a decent return with the minimum acceptable risk. If you own shares in one company then the risk and possibility of losing your money is greater than if the risk is spread.

It is a general rule that the lower the risk the lower the return. However, the converse holds true, the higher the risk the higher the return. For some people who invest in a single company the rewards can be big if the company does well. In truth what usually happens is that large investments in one company will not produce massive returns or result in loss of all ones investment. The shares will usually carry on rising marginally in the longer term.

Buying through Investments Trusts-Purchasing unit trusts

There are benefits connected to the purchase of unit trusts and investment trusts as opposed to individual shares. With trusts you get a spread of investments over a number of companies, cutting the danger of one of the companies going out of business.

Investment trusts

Investment trusts are companies which invest in other companies on behalf of investors. They are termed close-end funds because the number of shares on issue is fixed and does not fluctuate no matter how popular the fund may be. This sort of investment is convenient for small investors who do not have enough money to buy a lot of shares in different companies thereby spreading the risk. An investment trust will have its money spread across a lot of companies so problems with one company will usually be compensated by a boom in another company. Managers of investment trusts are professionals, so, at least in theory, they will do better than the average person. It is true to say that investment companies are as good as their managers so it is wise to pick a company with a good and known track record.

Most investment funds have a lot of money to invest and they will usually invest in blue chip shares, unless specifically set up to invest in a specific type of share.

The cost of the stockbroker is the same as it would be with other dealings and the government stamp duty and the price spread between buying and selling price remains the same.

Although investment trust managers do have a lot of say in the nature and type of investments, investors will also have some say in what goes on by buying the right investment trust shares. There are trusts specializing in the higher risk stock markets such as Budapest, Istanbul and Madrid (called emerging markets); there are some investing in the Pacific Rim and some concentrating in Japan; some go for small companies and some specialize in Europe and the United States and so on. The spread of investments can be very diverse indeed and managers of investment trusts tend to be more adventurous on the whole than managers of unit trusts.

Some trusts are split capital trusts which have a finite life during which one class of share gets all the income, and when it is wound up the other class of share gets the proceeds from selling off the holdings.

Trusts are quoted on the Stock Exchange so the share price can be tracked and also the asset value of the trust can be calculated. The asset value is comprised of the value of the shares that the trust is holding compared with the trusts own share price. One main reason that many are priced differently than their real value is that major investing institutions avoid trusts. Huge pension funds or insurance companies do not have to buy in to investment expertise as they normally have their own experts. Therefore trusts are used mainly by private investors.

Unit trusts

Unit trusts have the same advantage of spreading risk over a large number of companies and of having the portfolio of shares managed by professionals. However, instead of the units being quoted on the stock market as investment trusts are, investors deal directly with the management company. Therefore the paper issued has no secondary market. The investor cannot sell to anyone other than back to the management company. The market is seen from the manager's viewpoint:

it sells units at the offer price and buys them back at the lower 'bid' price, to give it a profit from the spread as well as the management charge. Many unit trust prices are published in quality papers.

These are called 'open-ended' funds, because they are the pooled resources of all investors. If more people want to get into a unit trust it will issue more paper to accommodate them. Unlike the price of investment trust shares, which is set by market demand and can get totally out of line with the market value the price of units is set strictly by the value of shares the trust owns.

Tracker funds
Tracker funds move with the main stock market index, in the U.K that is usually taken to be the FTSE 100. This type of fund is for the less adventurous investor who looks for a virtually risk free return.

Open-ended investment companies
Open Ended Investment companies or OEICs are placed midway between investment trusts and unit trusts. They are incorporated companies and issue shares, like investment companies. Like unit trusts the number of shares on issue depends on how much money investors want to put into the fund. When money is taken out and shares sold back, those shares are cancelled. The companies usually contain a number of shares segmented by specialism. This enables investors to pick the area they prefer and to switch from one fund to another with a minimum of administration and cost.

Advantages of pooled investments
Pooled investments reduce risk and are therefore a safer home for small investors. However, as they are safe they are unlikely to hit the outside chance of a high performer, as individual share speculators might.

As stated earlier, there are many different companies and a certain degree of research and knowledge is essential before committing. To be forewarned is to be forearmed. Quality newspapers will have regular league tables of performance. Be careful too with tables that are published showing performance. Obviously, tables can only look backwards to demonstrate past performance and it is the future that matters. Trusts can do very well, but it may be that they have done well in a sector that has expanded and is now contracting. Management charges for both investment trusts and unit trusts are usually high. One way of avoiding high charges is to opt for a U.S. mutual fund, which is the same as a unit trust and which has lower charges.

There is also the alternative of setting up your own investment vehicle which has become quite popular over the years. Investment clubs, described below, already very popular in the United States are growing more popular up in the U.K. Basically, a group of people together pool cash for investment in the stock market. The usual way is for each member to set aside a regular amount each month and decide where to invest it. This has the advantages of avoiding charges, spreading investments and also the social spin off. Also, the work of researching shares is spread amongst members.

Exchange traded funds

Exchange-traded funds, or ETFs, are investment companies that are legally classified as open-end companies or Unit Investment Trusts (UITs), but that differ from traditional open-end companies and UITs in the following respects:

- ETFs do not sell individual shares directly to investors and only issue their shares in large blocks (blocks of 50,000 shares, for example) that are known as "Creation Units."

- Investors generally do not purchase Creation Units with cash. Instead, they buy Creation Units with a basket of securities that generally mirrors the ETF's portfolio. Those who purchase Creation Units are frequently institutions.

- After purchasing a Creation Unit, an investor often splits it up and sells the individual shares on a secondary market. This permits other investors to purchase individual shares (instead of Creation Units).

- Investors who want to sell their ETF shares have two options: (1) they can sell individual shares to other investors on the secondary market, or (2) they can sell the Creation Units back to the ETF. In addition, ETFs generally redeem Creation Units by giving investors the securities that comprise the portfolio instead of cash. So, for example, an ETF invested in the stocks contained in the Dow Jones Industrial Average (DJIA) would give a redeeming shareholder the actual securities that constitute the DJIA instead of cash. Because of the limited redeemability of ETF shares,

ETFs are not considered to be—and may not call themselves—mutual funds.

An ETF, like any other type of investment company, will have a prospectus. All investors that purchase Creation Units receive a prospectus. Some ETFs may furnish an investor with a summary prospectus containing key information about the ETF instead of a long-form prospectus. If an investor receives a summary prospectus, the ETF's long-form prospectus will be available on an Internet Web site, and an investor can obtain a paper copy upon request and without charge. Some broker-dealers also deliver a prospectus to secondary market purchasers. ETFs that do not deliver a prospectus are required to give investors a document known as a Product Description, which summarizes key information about the ETF and explains how to obtain a prospectus. All ETFs will deliver a prospectus upon request. Before purchasing ETF shares, you should carefully read all of an ETF's available information, including its prospectus.

The websites of the New York Stock Exchange and NASDAQ provide more information about different types of ETFs and how they work. An ETF will have annual operating expenses and may also impose certain shareholders fees that are disclosed in the prospectus.

Investment clubs

Investment clubs are an alternative to funds managed by professionals and as a result can keep costs down. Investment clubs are a group of private investors who pool their money and decide collectively how it should be invested. There are now over 7,000 investment clubs in the U.K.

The ideal number of people in an investment club is usually between 4-20. If the membership exceeds 20 then HMRC will term the club a corporation and corporation tax will be payable. There are several stockbrokers, including major banks who have ready-made packages for investment clubs, such as Barclays and Nat West.

There is a specialist charity called pro-share which publishes a handbook on how to start an investment club. The advice contained in this handbook is very useful indeed because, although it is not absolutely necessary to have an in-depth knowledge of the stock market when joining an investment club it is at least useful to know something about the different sectors that you will be investing in.

For investors clubs there are model rules and constitutions that need to be adopted. As with all collective endeavours, from residents associations to enthusiasts clubs, rules and guidelines are essential. Investment club rules will set out, for example, how members can join and leave the club, a unit valuation system that is to be adopted, the decision making process, levels of monthly subscription, meetings, appointment of officers and so on. It is of the utmost importance that procedures are followed as disaster will almost certainly ensue. It is important to look at whether the club will run indefinitely, accumulating a portfolio or whether it has a specific life, say 5 years. An investor might be invited to join an existing club so it is important that these rules are already in place and that they are the right ones for you.

A few other tips. Only join in with people that you like and trust. Ensure that their objectives and goals are the same as yours or it could end in tears later down the line. The criteria for choosing investments varies widely from club to club but many will go for the riskier end of the market because the club membership is additional to a members own personal investments. Some investment clubs will go beyond the stock market and invest in property either directly or indirectly through another vehicle.

The main advice given to any club member or would-be member is not to invest in anything that you do not understand. Avoid the overly complex and riskier markets such as derivatives, unless you have an expert on board.

Most clubs invest a small sum, it could be under £80 per month, so this type of investing is just as much fun, and social, as it is serious money making. There are some investment clubs who have had runaway success but, on the whole it is for the smaller investor with other aims in mind.

The cost of dealing in shares as an individual

Share dealing can be expensive, particularly in Britain. It is the case that it is more expensive here than in many other countries, and also the whole process is more complex, at least for individual shareholders. True, there have been moves by high street banks and other companies to make the process more transparent but it is still the case that small shareholders find the process rather confusing. It is also the case that small shareholders are still perceived to be a nuisance, because they deal in small amounts of money which cost just as much to transact as larger deals.

Commission

Commission paid to stockbrokers constitutes the main cost of dealing in shares. Commissions vary depending on the nature of the work and the type of broker. Rates of commission can vary anything from £5 per transaction up to £20 with commission on a sliding scale above the minimum depending on the value of the transaction. An order of £2,000 might cost 1.5% with the rate falling the higher the transaction. There can also be a one-off charge of at least £10 for joining Crest, the UK stock exchanges registry of share holdings. There are several internet sites, such as www.fool.co.uk which provide information about brokers commissions. It is worth looking at this site before going ahead.

The spread

As well as brokers commission there is the cost of trading. Shares are like other commodities, the costs of buying and selling shares will differ. This difference is known as the 'spread'. Spread varies with risk. Big companies listed on the FTSE 100, such as Barclays, British Airways etc have huge market capitalisations and many shareholders with regular deals every day so would have a narrow spread of say 1-1.5%. A company with few shareholders and little trade would have a spread of up to 10%. The result is that for shareholders of small companies the shares have to rise even higher to realise a profit. There is lots of free advice concerning shares. However, it is true to say that for the small, first time investor even free advice can be confusing and misleading, given that this advice is often slanted in favour of whoever gives it. It is therefore advisable to use a stockbroker who is seasoned and knows the markets well.

For those with a larger share portfolio it is possible to sub-contract out the management. The stockbroker managing the portfolio will advise on investments but leave the final decision to the investor. The value of portfolios has to be high however, and this will not usually be the route for small investors. In addition to portfolio management there is discretionary management where a fee is paid to an advisor to provide advice on shares and also the timing of share purchase. The fee paid is quite high, or is based on a percentage and is therefore only useful for those with bigger portfolios.

Income tax

Another consideration to take into account, after everyone has taken their cut, is that of the ever-present HMRC. The government will take its cut by imposing a tax called stamp duty at the rate of .5% on the value of every deal that has used taxed income. The French and German governments do not impose such a tax therefore money can be saved by investing through these exchanges.

Buying shares

The process of buying shares has become markedly easier over the last few decades. In fact, many people have acquired shares through privatisations and through building societies becoming banks, and have not had to use a stockbroker. However, if people want to buy shares in the usual way there are several routes.

The first one is finding a stockbroker. Years ago, this was out of the reach of the small investor. Most stockbrokers operated within exclusive circles. Many did not want to be bothered with the small investor who knew very little, if anything about the markets. Banks have entered the arena with share dealing services and so has a new breed of transaction only brokers (who buy and sell but do not offer advice). However, more and more information is becoming available, through the internet and in newspapers. There has been a trend to present information in a plain English way and the information regarding shares is no different. Finding a broker over the internet is probably the easiest way to get started.

The internet has undermined the closed nature of share dealing and there are a large number of independent companies, most of which are members of The Association Of Private Client Investment Managers and Stockbrokers (see useful addresses). Many have their own web sites.

There are three main types of broker, each offering a differing array of services: execution-only brokers; advisory brokers; discretionary brokers.

Execution only brokers

Execution-only brokers will simply handle the sale or purchase of shares at your request, whether this is carried out online or on the phone. They do not offer investment advice. The firms computer routes your order to the market where the shares are trading and it will simply execute your order at the best possible price. The broker will receive a commission on each transaction.

Advisory brokers

As the name suggests, an advisory broker will offer the best advice and strategies for you to increase the value of your investment portfolio and achieve your investment aims. This type of broker will try to get to know you and to gain a clearer idea of your aims. An advisory broker will be more expensive than an execution only broker, because of the more intensive nature of their service, but if you take advantage of the expert advice on offer then it will be worthwhile.

Discretionary brokers

This type of broker will have written authority from you or someone acting on your behalf to decide what securities can be bought and sold on your account.

For most new investors who may not be very knowledgeable about the markets or investing, it is generally safer to go with an advisory broker who can help you through the maze and also help to maximise the value of your investments.

People who think that they need help and advice can go to one of the big high street financial institutions with branches round the country. They can also seek out a good local firm that is experienced in the needs of small investors. The best way to find such a firm is by recommendation (like a lot of things) or you can go to the Association of Private Client Investment Managers and Stockbrokers.

Before picking a broker, ask questions such as how easily contactable are they and other terms and conditions.

****

16

Internet broking

Internet broking has, like many other activities on the internet, grown massively. The internet has a lot of real advantages. Investors can place an order whenever they feel ready and can do it from any place any time. In addition, an enormous amount of information is available online to assist with decision making.

Dealing on the internet can also be cheaper. It is possible to deal over the net for a flat fee of around £10, although this varies (see below). This is important for those who plan to be active investors and to whom the fees paid are crucial to profit margins. One Paris based research outfit called Blue Sky reckons that the four best value online brokers are all German.

The table overleaf shows 13 brokers who figure in the top lists of Internet share dealers. For an up to date list of the top 40 brokers you should go to www.the-international-investor.com. This is a comprehensive site which will also explain the terminology behind internet investing.

See overleaf

Name	Standard account fees	Frequent trader rate	Charge per trade
Halifax www.halifax.co.uk	No fee		£12.95
Hargreaves Lansdowne www.hl.co.uk		£8.95 £5.95	£11.95
		£4.95	£9.90
		£9.75	£11.95
Sippdeal www.sippdeal.co.uk			£5
Saga www.saga.co.uk	£18.75 per Qtr		£12.50
Self trade www.selftrade.co.uk	£10.50 Qtr	£6	£12.50
Club Finance www. clubfinance.co.uk	0.24%	£0.50	£12.50
TD Direct Investing www.tddirectinvesting.co.uk	£24 half year inactivity fee	£8.95 £5.95	£12.50
AJ Bell You Invest www.youinvest.co.uk		£4.95	£9.95
Interactive investor www.ii.co.uk	£20 Qtr	£5	£10
Saxo Capital Markets www.saxomarkets.com	12% per year with 60 euro minimum		Varies
Share centre www.	£1.80 per month		Varies

One acknowledged problem with the web is that it is hard to get a picture of the reliability of the firm that you are dealing with. The web is largely faceless so there are risks of various sorts, such as hacking into your data and so on. Online trading does not generate a share certificate. The shares are registered to the new owner but it is still computerised and the broker will hold the title to them in a nominee account. This can mean that the investor cannot easily change allegiance to another broker.

To join an online stockbroker, you need to get on to a website and follow instructions for registering. Almost all will require cash deposited with the brokerage. Interest is paid on this money at a low rate. When signing on you register a password which provides secure access for the investor.

If you want to invest in the US you might want to go through a US based broker. These brokers are cheaper than European counterparts.

There are two sorts of dealing online: one is to e-mail an instruction to a broker who will execute it via his trading screen. In theory he can do that within 15 seconds and within 15 minutes the deal can be confirmed. The other method is called real time dealing in which the investor connects directly to the stock market dealing system.

Normally, when the instruction is given, the broker will 'transact at best'-buy at the lowest available price and sell at the highest. The broker can be set a limit-the maximum at which you are prepared to buy or the minimum price below which you are not prepared to sell. Usually, such limits last for 24 hours although can be longer.

Once the transaction is complete the broker sends a contract note detailing the deal and how much money is to change hands. It may take some time to receive the share certificate but the important element is the presence on the share register.

In the previous chapters, I have explained the workings of the Stock market and also how companies raise capital on the stock market. Also, we have looked at vehicles for investing in stocks and shares and also the costs of purchasing shares.

In the following chapters we will look at the nature of information that is presented in newspapers, in particular the Financial Times, and how to interpret that data. Following that we will look at companies in more depth and then at the situation concerning share purchase, dividends and taxation.

****

17

Interpreting Financial Information- Reading the Papers

It is very important to be able to interpret the range of information about stocks and shares, and company information, that is printed in newspapers each day. The frequency and extent of the information will differ slightly depending on the newspaper. In this chapter we will concentrate on the UK equities market as this is the area which most small investors will be interested in.

As we have seen, an equity is another word for a share or stake in a company. The owner of the share will, hopefully, receive a dividend annually and will enjoy capital appreciation. The equity markets in the UK trade shares across a wide range of companies, from established and stable blue chip companies to the more high-risk ventures.

Although many newspapers do provide information concerning the equities market, and the information is the same, in this chapter we will concentrate on the best known paper dealing with financial information, the Financial Times, or FT.

The financial times gives in depth daily coverage of the equities market and this consists of the following elements:

- A report daily of the most interesting trading features of the stock market.
- The share price of individual companies.
- Various financial ratios
- Reports on individual companies
- Stock market indices indicating overall progress of equity share prices.

The London Stock Exchange Market Information
The London stock exchange is just about the most comprehensive record of UK market statistics available to the general public and covers around 3,000 shares. The LSS is divided into different industrial classifications. The share service covers companies listed both on the main stock market and also the Alternative Investment market (AIM), discussed earlier.

The market information is published in the FT from Tuesday to Saturday in the companies and markets section. The table below indicates the way the information is presented.

Aerospace and defence

Notes	Price	Change	High	Low	Yield	P/E	Vol 000's
BAE Systems	229	-2.5	291.5	199.25	3.3	16.8	35.419
Chenning	490.5	-1	491.5	373.5	1.9	13.4	79
Cobham	1367	-32	1460	1237	2.3	14.5	370
Hampson	21.75	-1.5	30	18.25	-78.5	.5	262
Meggitt	297.5	-3.25	300.25	208	2.4	19.0	2756

The symbols below will be indicated alongside shares and can be interpreted as follows:

'A' alongside a share name indicates that it carries no voting rights.
♣ indicates that investors can get a free copy of the company's latest reports and accounts.

♥ this indicates that the stock is not listed in the UK.

♠ this indicates an unregulated collective investment scheme.

Xd means that the recently declared dividend will still be paid to the previous owner of the share.

Xr indicates the same for a rights issue- i.e. the buyer will not be acquiring the right to subscribe to the new issue of shares.

Xc means that the buyer does not get a scrip issue of shares which the company is issuing in lieu of a dividend.

Interpreting the figures

Interpreting the figures is largely self- explanatory.

1. The first column – notes - lists the company name.
2. The second column – price – shows the average (or mid price) of the best buying and selling prices quoted by market makers at the

close of market on the previous day, the close being 4.30pm. If trading in the share has been suspended for some reason then this is denoted by a symbol and the price quoted is the price at suspension. The letters 'xfd' following a price mean ex-dividend and indicate that a dividend has been announced but this will not be available to new purchasers.

3. Price change. This will be plus or minus depending on the movement of the shares. This column will give the change in closing price compared with the end of the previous day.

4. Previous price movements. The fourth and fifth columns show the highest and lowest prices recorded for the stock during the past 12 months.

5. Dividend yield. The sixth column shows the percentage return on the share. It is calculated by dividing the dividend by the current share price.

6. Price earning ratio (P/E). The seventh column is the market price of the share divided by the companies earnings (profits) per share in the last 12 month trading period. Yields and P/E ratios move in opposite directions: if the share price rises, since the dividend remains the same, the dividend yield falls; at the same time, since the earnings per share are constant, the P/E ratio rises.

7. The last column, 8, deals with the number of shares traded the previous day rounded to the nearest 1,000.

How to use the information effectively

The first indicator to look at is that of price. The price is the current price of a share. This needs to be looked at in conjunction with the 52 week high and low in order to get some kind of historical perspective of performance of the company.

The prices quoted are the mid-prices between the bid or buying price and the offer or selling price at which market makers will trade. The difference between bid and offer is known as the spread and it represents market makers profit on any given transaction. The implication of the spread is that investors will only be able to buy at a higher price and sell at a lower price than that quoted in the newspaper.

Volume is an indication of the liquidity of a stock, or how easy it is to buy and sell. High volume is much more preferable than low volume but take into account the fact that smaller companies are traded much less heavily than larger companies. Volumes will also be higher when a company makes an announcement.

The dividend yield is a reflection of the way that the market values a company. If the company is thought to have a high growth rate and is deemed to be a secure business, then its current dividend yield will be low, since the scope for increasing dividends in the future is average.

The dividend, to some degree, is an arbitrary figure, decided at the whim of a company. The figure for the yield is not always a good indicator of the vale of a share. Price/earnings ratios are generally better as they are independent of arbitrary corporate decisions.

Price/earnings ratios are the most commonly used tool of stock market analysis. Essentially, they compare a company's share price with its annual earnings, indicating the number of years that it would take for the company, at its current earning power, to earn an amount equal to its market value. Shares are often described as selling at a number times earnings or on a multiple. In general terms, the higher a company's ratio the more highly rated it is by the market. High price/earnings ratios are usually associated with low yields. A high ratio suggests a growth stock and is, like a low yield, an indicator of an investment where capital growth might be more important than income.

Evaluation of weekly performance

Monday's edition of the financial times will indicate weekly changes in share prices. The column will look as follows:

Weekly tables

1	2	3	4	5	6	7	8
Notes	Price	WK% Change	Div	Div Cov	Mcap £m	Last XD	City line
BAE Systems	♣288.25	4.3	9.5	1.8	9,262	20.4	1890
Chenning	476.5	1.3	9.4	3.9	138.6	11.5	2116

The weekly column indicates:

Notes-the name of the company

1. Price with relevant symbol
2. The weeks price change as a percentage
3. Dividend – the dividends paid in the last financial year
4. Dividend cover - the ratio of profits to dividends, calculated by dividing the earnings per share by the dividend per share. This indicates how many times a company's dividend to ordinary shareholders could be paid out of net profits

5. Market capitalisation – this is an indication of the stock market valuation of the company in millions of pounds. It is calculated, as we saw earlier, by multiplying the numbers of shares by their market price.
6. Ex-dividend date – this is the last date on which a share went ex-dividend, expressed as a day and month unless a dividend has not been paid for some time. On and after this date, the rights to the last announced dividend remain with the seller of the stock. The share register is frozen on the xd date and the dividend will be paid to the people on the register at that time. Until it is paid, buyers of the share will not receive the next payment due.
7. Cityline – the FT Cityline code by which real-time shares are available over the telephone by calling 0906 003 or 0906 843 plus the four-digit code for any given share. This telephone information service is designed primarily for investors wanting to keep track of their own investments or the activity of the UK and world stock markets at any point.

The key information from this listing is that of dividend cover. This indicates how safe the dividend is from future cuts. The higher the figure the better able a company will be to maintain its dividends if profits fall.

Other share dealings
Financial times share price coverage is expanded on a weekly basis on ft.com to cover dealings in securities that are not included in the standard share information service. Information is provided on name and stock type plus price.

Trading volume
The back page of the companies and markets section has a useful reference table with the trading volume and basic price information for the constituents of the FTSE Index, the index of the top 100 UK companies. This will deal with the largest capitalised and most actively traded stocks.

Trading volume, price and change in stocks are indicated in this table. Trading volume is an indication of the liquidity of a stock. The higher the figure, the easier it will be to buy or sell significant quantities of stock without having a major impact on its price.

The FT carries three other lists for quick reference on share price movements.

Share rises and falls

This table, shown daily, shows how many securities rose, fell and stayed at the same price level during the previous trading session. It is broken down into nine different categories of security and shows how movements in the main share price indices were reflected in trading across the various market divisions.

Highs and lows

This table shows which shares have, on the previous day reached new high or low points for the past 12 months. The highs and lows table highlights company's that are moving against the general trends of their sector.

Main movers

This table will indicate the stocks that had the biggest percentage rise and falls the previous day. It will indicate the name of the company, the closing price, the days change as a price and percentage.

Winners and losers

Saturday's FT includes a table of the FTSE winners and losers. This lists the top and bottom six performing companies over the previous week in three sectors (the FTSE 100, the FTSE 250 and the FTSE SmallCap sector). Included will be their latest price, percentage price change on the week and change on the start of the year. It also lists the six top and bottom performing industry sectors.

There are price tables for unit trusts and gilts. Gilts are normally split into short, medium and long-dated. There are also two undated ones and index-linked stocks. Foreign governments also issue bonds that are listed.

Indices

Newspapers also print information for the movement of specific industrial sectors, plus some describing the type of share. These are then aggregated to form wider industrial indices such as Basic Industries, General Industrials, 650, All Share and so on. The Financial Times produces a full list of the FTSE indices compiled and calculated under formulae developed by actuaries.

Every stock market has its indices to show movements in the market as a whole. Different papers report different selections of these. As mentioned previously, some of the better known ones are the Dow Jones, Nasdaq, Standard and Poor's, Toronto 300. Nikkei, Hang Seng, Dax for Germany, CAC40 for France and the Toronto Composite Index. There is also a table for the highest volumes of trade.

Papers such as the Financial Times will also provide invaluable editorials and views of experts which should be studied carefully as they are quite often right and can steer investors away from potential problems.

****

18

Shares and Taxation

The area of tax and share dealing has always been a bone of contention. However, it is an important area and must be understood.

Dividends

Dividends on shares are usually paid net of tax and the voucher that comes with the payment notification will contain details of a tax credit. People who do not normally pay income tax cannot reclaim the tax already paid on the dividend, and people paying tax at the basic rate need pay no further tax on the income.

People who pay tax below an income of £31,685, which is the basic limit (2014-15) pay 10%. People who pay tax at the higher rate or below (up to £150,000) have to pay at 32.5% of the gross, though the credit detailed on the slip is set off against this. Essentially, about a quarter of the net dividend is due in tax for higher rate payers. For those above the higher rate the limit is 37.5%.

Scrip issues of shares in lieu of dividend are treated in a similar way. There is no tax to standard rate payers and the higher rates are assumed to have had a 10% tax credit.

If the company buys back shares then the tax situation is the same as a dividend.

See below for a current breakdown of dividend tax rates.

Dividend tax rates

Dividend tax rates 2014 to 2015

Dividend income in relation to the basic rate or higher rate tax bands	Tax rate applied after deduction of Personal Allowance and any Blind Person's Allowance
Dividend income at or below the £31,865 basic rate tax limit	10%
Dividend income at or below the £150,000 higher rate tax	32.5%

Dividend income in relation to the basic rate or higher rate tax bands limit	Tax rate applied after deduction of Personal Allowance and any Blind Person's Allowance
Dividend income above the higher rate tax limit	37.5%

It doesn't matter whether you get dividends from a company, unit trusts or open-ended investment company, as all dividends are taxed the same way.

How dividends are paid

When you get your dividend you also get a voucher that shows:

- the dividend paid - the amount you received

- the amount of associated 'tax credit' - see next section

If you have agreed to get your dividends paid electronically you may get your dividend voucher in paper or electronic form.

Understanding the dividend tax credit

Companies pay you dividends out of profits on which they have already paid - or are due to pay - tax. The tax credit takes account of this and is available to the shareholder to offset against any Income Tax that may be due on their dividend income.

When adding up your overall taxable income you need to include the sum of the dividend(s) received and the tax credit(s). This income is called your dividend income.

How tax credits are worked out

The dividend you are paid represents 90 per cent of your 'dividend income'. The remaining 10 per cent of the dividend income is made up of the tax credit. Put another way, the tax credit represents 10 per cent of the dividend income.

Dividend income at or below the £31,865 basic rate tax limit

See overleaf.

Dividend paid to you (represents 90% of the dividend income)	Tax credit (10% of the dividend income)	Dividend income (dividend paid plus tax credit)
£63	£7	£70
£54	£6	£60
£90	£10	£100

Paying tax on dividend income

If you pay tax at the basic rate

You have no tax to pay on your dividend income because the tax liability is 10 per cent - the same amount as the tax credit - as shown in the earlier tables.

If you pay tax at the higher rate

You pay a total of 32.5 per cent tax on dividend income inclusive of tax credit where this falls above the basic rate Income Tax limit (£31.865 for the 2014-15 tax year). In practice, however, you owe only 25 per cent of the dividend paid to you after the tax credit has been taken into account.

If you pay tax at the additional rate

Since the 2010-11 tax year you pay a total of 37.5 per cent tax on dividend income that exceeds the higher rate Income Tax limit (currently £150,000). But because the first 10 per cent of the tax due on your dividend income is already covered by the tax credit, in practice you owe only 36.1 per cent of the dividend paid to you.

Note that dividend income, like savings income, is taxed after your non-savings income - for example, wages and self-employment profit - at your highest tax rate. For example, if it falls both sides of the £31.865 basic rate tax limit, it will be taxed partly at 10 per cent (and covered by the tax credit) and partly at 32.5 per cent (less the 10 per cent tax credit).

Declaring dividend income on your Self Assessment tax return

If you normally complete a tax return you'll need to show the dividend income on it. If you don't complete a tax return, but you have higher rate of tax to pay on your dividend income, you should contact HMRC.

Can you claim the tax credit if you don't normally pay tax?

No. You can't claim the 10 per cent tax credit, even if your taxable income is less than your Personal Allowance and you don't pay tax. This is because Income Tax hasn't been deducted from the dividend paid to you - you have simply been given a 10 per cent credit against any Income Tax due.

Capital profits

A profit on the sale of shares is liable to tax for profits above the basic tax-free allowance. Capital gains tax is only a problem for those people who deal in large amounts of stocks. Windfall shares received from demutualized building societies or insurance companies are counted as having cost nothing and anything made from their sale is counted as a capital gain, unless they have been put into a tax sheltering scheme such as an ISA.

There is a tapered tax relief however, so holding a share for a long time will reduce the tax liability. If the shares were bought before April 1998 the price rise can be adjusted for inflation before tax is payable. Dealing costs in buying and selling are allowable against the total gain and there is also an allowance for part paid shares. Gifts between spouses are tax free, so a portfolio can be adjusted to obtain the maximum allowance.

Losses made from selling shares in the same tax year can be set off against the profit. If any of the companies go bankrupt, the shares are seen to have been sold off at that date for nothing and the capital loss from the purchase can also be set off against any gains made.

Share schemes

Receiving shares from an employer counts as pay and is subject to income tax. If the employee buys the shares at a discount to the market price, the employee will pay tax on the discount. Under approved profit-sharing schemes the company can allocate tax-free shares to workers, although there are many rules attached to this.

Enterprise investment schemes

Investment in newly issued shares of an unlisted company can be set off against income tax at a reduced rate, but the full relief both in income and capital gains taxes comes only if the shares are held for years. Losses can be set off against either capital gains or income. Capital gains can also be deferred by rolling the investment over: after selling the proceeds from one investment it can be invested in another and no tax paid until the investment is realised.

Venture capital trusts

This is a version of Enterprise Investment Schemes. Tax breaks are almost the same but the investment is in a quoted financial vehicle, which will invest the cash in a variety of businesses. The risk is therefore reduced by spreading over a number of ventures.

The above is very brief and for more in depth advice you should refer to an accountant experienced in these matters.

****

19

Pensions and Planning for the Future

Planning for the future

The main principle with all pension provision is that the sooner you start saving money in a pension plan the more that you will have at retirement. The later that you leave it the less you will have or the more expensive that it will be to create a fund adequate enough for your needs.

In order to gauge your retirement needs, you will need to have a clear idea of your lifestyle, or potential lifestyle in retirement. This is not something that you can plan, or want to plan, at a younger age but the main factor is that the more that you have the easier life will be. There are two main factors which currently underpin retirement:

- Improved health and longevity-we are living longer and we have better health so therefore we are more active
- People are better off-improved state and company pensions

Sources of pension and other retirement income

Government statistics indicate that there is a huge gap between the poorest and richest pensioners in the United Kingdom. No surprise there. The difference between the richest fifth of single pensioners and the poorest fifth is about £400 per week. The poorest fifth of pensioners in the UK are reliant mainly on state benefits whilst the wealthier groups have occupational incomes and also personal investment incomes. The tables below indicates the disparity between the richest and poorest socio-economic groups:

TYPE OF PENSIONER HOUSEHOLD

See Overleaf.

Income per week Single   Couple

			603					1451
		327					669	
	256					497		
216					379			
162				274				

Poorest Next 5th Middle 5th Next 5th Richest 5th Poorest 5th Next 5th Middle 5th Next 5th Richest 5th
Source: The Pensioners Income Series 2012-2013.

Income sources of poorest and richest pensioners (Single and couple pensioners average)

Poorest	Richest
Occupational Pensions 9%	Occupational pensions 29.5%
Personal Pensions 3%	Personal Pensions 4.5%
Investment income 3%	Investment income 14%
Earnings 5%	Earnings 32%
Other 1%	Other 1%
Benefit Income 79%	Benefit Income 19%

Source: The Pensioners Income Series 2012-2013

The above illustrates that those in the poorest and wealthiest bands have a wide gap in income, in particular in the areas of earnings and investments. The richest have managed to ensure that there is enough money in the pot to cater for retirement. Those in the lower income bands rely heavily on state pensions and other benefits. For more information on the Pensioner Income Series you should go to www.gov.uk/government/collection/pensioners-income-series-statistics-july-2014. There is a whole array of comparisons and general information, most of it quite interesting.

When attempting to forecast for future pension needs, there are a number of factors which need to be taken into account:

- Your income needs in retirement and how much of that income you can expect to derive from state pensions
- How much pension that any savings you have will produce
- How long you have to save for
- Projected inflation

1. Income needs in retirement

This is very much a personal decision and will be influenced by a number of factors, such as ongoing housing costs, care costs, projected lifestyle etc. The main factor is that you have enough to live on comfortably. In retirement you will probably take more holidays and want to enjoy your free time. This costs money so your future planning should take into account all your projected needs and costs. The next chapter includes a few calculations about future needs. When calculating future needs, all sources of income should be taken into account.

2. What period to save over

The obvious fact is that, the longer period that you save over then the more you will build up and hence the more that you will have in retirement. As time goes on savings are compounded and the value of the pot goes up. One thing is for certain and that is if you leave it too late then you will have to put away a large slice of your income to produce a decent pension. If you plan to retire at an early age then you will need to save more to produce the same benefits. We will discuss saving arrangements further on in this book.

3. Inflation

As prices rise, so your money buys you less. This is the main effect of inflation and to maintain the same level of spending power you will need to save more as time goes on. Many forms of retirement plans will include a calculation for inflation. Currently, inflation is at a low level, 0.3% per annum (January 2015). However, history shows that the effects of inflation can be corrosive, having risen above 25% per annum in the past. Hopefully, this is now under control

****

20

How Much Income is needed in Retirement-Planning Ahead

For most people, retirement is a substantial part of life, probably lasting a couple of decades or more. It follows that ensuring your financial security in retirement requires some forward planning. Developing a plan calls for a general review of your current finances and careful consideration of how you can build up your savings to generate the retirement income that you need.

There are five distinct stages to planning your retirement which are summarised below.

Stage 1-this involves checking first that other aspects of your basic finances are in good shape. Planning for retirement generally means locking away your money for a long time. Once invested it is usually impossible to get pension savings back early, even if in an emergency. It is therefore essential that you have other more accessible savings available for emergencies and that you do not have any problem debts that could tip you into a financial crisis. You must then weigh up saving for retirement against other goals that are more pressing, such as making sure that your household would be financially secure if you were unable to work because of illness or the main breadwinner dies.

Stage 2-You need to decide how much income you might need when you retire. There is a table below which might help you in calculating this.

Stage 3- Check how much pension that you have built up so far.

Stage 4-Compare your amount from stage 3 with your target income from stage 2.

Stage 5-Review your progress once a year and/or if your circumstances change.

It is a fact that many people need far less in retirement than when actively working. The expenses that exist when working, such as mortgage payments, children and work related expenses do not exist when retired. The average household between 30-49 spends £473 per week and £416 between 50-64. This drops to £263 per week between 65 to 74 and even lower in later retirement (Expenditure and Food Survey 2012).

However, as might be expected, expenditure on health care increases correspondingly with age. Whilst the state may help with some costs the individual still has to bear a high proportion of expenditure on health related items.

When calculating how much money you will need in retirement, it is useful to use a table in order to list your anticipated expenses as follows:

1. Everyday needs

Item	Annual Total £
Food and other	
Leisure (newspapers etc)	
Pets	
Clothes	
Other household items	
Gardening	
General expenses	

Home expenses

Mortgage/rent	
Service charges/repairs	
Insurance	
Council tax	
Water and other utilities	
Telephone	
TV licence other charges (satellite)	
Other expenses (home help)	

Leisure and general entertainment

Hobbies	
Eating out	
Cinema/theatre	
Holidays	
Other luxuries (smoking/drinking	

Transport

Car expenses	
Car hire	
Petrol etc	
Bus/train fares	

Health

Dental charges	
Optical expenses	
Medical insurance	
Care insurance	
Other health related expenses	

Anniversaries/birthdays etc

Children/grandchildren	
Relatives other than children	
Christmas	
Charitable donations	
Other expenses	

Savings and loans

General savings	
Saving for later retirement	
Other savings	
Loan repayments	

Other

The above should give you an idea of the amounts that you will need per annum to live well. Obviously, you should plan for a monthly income that will meet those needs. You should also take account of income tax on your retirement incomes.

The impact of inflation

When you are planning for many years ahead, it is essential to take account of the effects of inflation. Currently, at the time of writing in 2015, we are in a period of low inflation, 0.3% largely due to low oil prices. As prices rise over the years, the money we will have will buy less and less. For example, in the extreme case, if prices double then a fixed amount of money will buy only half as much. The higher the rate of inflation,. The more you have to save to reach your income target. the table below will give you an idea of the changes in rates of inflation over the last ten years. The ONS supplies figures to 2013.

Yr	J	F	M	A	M	J	Jul	A	S	O	N	D	Ann
2013	2.7	2.8	2.8	2.4	2.7	2.9	2.8	2.7	2.7	2.2	2.1	2	2.56
2012	3.6	3.4	3.5	3	2.8	2.4	2.6	2.5	2.2	2.6	2.6	2.7	2.8
2011	4	4.3	4.1	4.5	4.5	4.2	4.5	4.5	5.2	5	4.8	4.2	4.5
2010	3..4	3	3.4	3.7	3.3	3.2	3.1	3.1	3	3.1	3.2	3.7	3.3
2009	3	3.1	2.9	2.3	2.2	1.8	1.7	1.5	1.1	1.5	1.9	2.8	2.2
2008	2.2	2.5	2.4	3	3.3	3.8	4.4	4.8	5.2	4.5	4.1	3.1	3.6
2007	2.7	2.8	3.1	2.8	2..5	2.4	1.9	1.7	1.7	2	2.1	2.1	2.3
2006	1.9	2.1	1.8	2	2.2	2.5	2.4	2.5	2.4	2.5	3	3	2.3
2005	1.6	1.6	2	1.9	1.9	1.9	2.4	2.3	2.4	2.3	1.9	1.9	2
2004	1.4	1.3	1.1	1.1	1.4	1.7	1.3	1.3	1.1	1.2	1.6	1.6	1.3
2003	1.4	1.6	1.6	1.5	1.3	1	1.4	1.4	1.5	1.4	1.2	1.2	1.4

Office of National Statistics 2015.

Some pension schemes give you automatic protection against inflation, but many don't and it is largely up to you to decide what protection to build into your planning. The first step is to be aware what effect inflation might have. Fortunately, pension statements and projections these days must all be adjusted for inflation so that figures you are given are expressed in today's money. This gives you an idea of the standard of living you might expect and helps you assess the amount that you need to save. Providers of non-pension investments (such as unit trusts and investment trusts (see later chapters) do not have to give you statements and projections adjusted for inflation. If you use these other investments for your retirement then you will have to make your own adjustments. You can do this using the table below.

Value in today's money of £1,000 you receive in the future
Average rate of inflation

Number of years until you receive the money	2.5% a year	5% a year	7.5% a year	10% a year
5	£884	£784	£697	£621
10	£781	£614	£485	£386
15	£690	£481	£338	£239
20	£610	£377	£235	£149
25	£539	£295	£164	£92
30	£477	£231	£114	£57
35	£421	£181	£80	£36
40	£372	£142	£55	£22
45	£329	£111	£39	£14
50	£291	£87	£39	£9

The above should be a good guide. If you require more detailed forecasting you can go to www.ons.gov.uk (Office of National Statistics).

****

21

Sources Of Pension Savings-Options for Retirement

1. The state pension

We will be elaborating on the state pension further in chapter 5. The state pension system is based on contributions, the payments made by an individual today funds today's pension payments and for those who are young the future contributions will foot their pension bill. Therefore, the state pension system is not a savings scheme it is a pay-as-you-go system.

Pensions are a major area of government spending and are becoming more and more so. Protecting pensions against inflationary increases have put pressure on respective governments, along with the introduction of a second tier-pension, the state second pension (S2P). This replaced SERPS. The problems of pension provision are set to increase with the numbers of older people outnumbering those in active work, leading to an imbalance in provision. The biggest dilemma facing the government, and future governments, is the problem of convincing people to save for their pensions, therefore taking some of the burden off the state.

Those most at risk in terms of retirement poverty are the lower earners, who quite often do not build up enough contributions to gain a state pension, those who contribute to a state pension but cannot save enough to contribute to a private scheme and disabled people who cannot work or carers who also cannot work. The above is not an exclusive list. The government has recognised the difficulties faced by these groups and have introduced the state second pension and pension credits.

Pension credits

Pension credits began life in October 2003. The credit is designed to top up the resources of pensioners whose income is low. The pension credit has two components: a guarantee credit and a saving credit. The guarantee credit is available to anyone over a qualifying age (equal to women's state pension age-see further on) whose income is less than a set amount called the minimum guarantee. The guarantee will bring income up to £148.36 for a single person and £226.50 for a couple (including same sex couples) (2014-2015). The minimum guarantee is higher for certain categories of disabled people and carers.

The savings credit

You can only claim savings credit if you or your partner are aged 65 or over. It's intended as a modest "reward" if you've provided yourself with a retirement income over and above the basic retirement pension.

Savings credit is calculated by the Pension Service, which checks whether you're entitled to guarantee credit, then makes a further calculation based on the information that you've provided about your income and capital. You don't have to do any calculations yourself. You may qualify for savings credit if your income is over the "savings threshold". The savings threshold is £120.35 a week for a single person and £192 a week for a couple. If your income is equal to or below these thresholds, you won't get any savings credit. This won't affect any guarantee credit you get.

The maximum savings credit you can get is £16.80 a week if you're single and £20.70 a week if you're married or living with a partner.

The income taken into account for savings credit is the same as for guarantee credit, but various types of income are now ignored. These are Working Tax Credit, contribution-based Employment and Support Allowance, Incapacity Benefit, contribution-based Jobseeker's Allowance, Severe Disablement Allowance, Maternity Allowance and maintenance payments made to you (child maintenance is always ignored).

If your income is still over the savings threshold, the Pension Service works out your entitlement to savings credit.

If you get guarantee credit, your savings credit payment is determined by how much your income exceeds the savings threshold. The payment given is 60% of the difference between the two figures, up to a maximum of £16.80 a week for a single person and £20.70 a week if you're married or living with a partner.

If you don't qualify for guarantee credit, you can still get savings credit at a reduced rate to reflect the fact that your income exceeds the minimum level the law says you need to live on. The same steps as above are taken to work out your entitlement, but the Pension Service will also calculate how much your income is above the appropriate minimum guarantee used for guarantee credit. Your savings credit award will be reduced by 40% of the difference.

Guarantee Credit

The Guarantee Credit element provides a guarantee of a minimum level of weekly income for single people (£148.35) and couples (£226.50). The individual applying must be over the qualifying age (see below for definition), although their spouse can be younger.

Before 6 April 2010, the qualifying age for the Guarantee Credit was 60. Since 6 April 2010, the qualifying age for the Guarantee Credit has started rising gradually to age 65 in line with the increase to women's state pension age (and then later to 66, 67 and 68).

The over 80 pension

This is a non-contributory pension for people aged 80 or over with little or no state pension. If you are 80 or over, not getting or getting a reduced state pension because you have not paid enough National Insurance contributions (NI) and are currently living in England, Scotland or Wales and have been doing so for a total of 10 years or more in any continuous period of 20 years before or after your 80th birthday, you could claim the over 80 pension. The maximum amount of the over 80 state pension that you can get is 60% of the full state pension. This is currently £67.80 per week (2014/15).

2. Personal Pension Arrangements

Occupational pensions

We discuss occupational pension schemes in more depth later in this book. Briefly, occupational pension schemes are a very important source of income. They are also one of the best ways to pay into a pension scheme as the employer has to contribute a significant amount to the pot. Over the years the amounts paid into occupational pension schemes has increased significantly. Although there have been a number of incidences of occupational schemes being wound up this is relatively small and they remain a key source of retirement income.

From October 2012, it has been compulsory for employers to provide an occupational pension scheme. For the first time, employers are obliged to:

- enrol most of their workforce into a pension scheme; and
- make employer pension contributions

This will affect all employers in the UK, regardless of the number of individuals that they employ. Anyone who is classed as a 'worker' for National Minimum Wage purposes is included in the new pension regime.

This will be introduced in stages, and each employer will be given a 'staging date' determined by how many employees they have as at April 1st 2012. These will fall into the following periods:

See overleaf.

	Staging starting date	Staging end date
120,000 or more	1 Oct 12	1 Feb 14
250-119,999	1 Nov 12	1 April 2015
50-249 employees	1 April 2014	1 April 2015
Less than 50 employees	1 June 2015	1 April 2017
New employers from 1 April 2012	1 May 2017	1 February 2018

The above table provides a summary. Specific staging dates can be found at the Pensions Regulator website: www.thepensionsregulator.gov.uk/employers/staging-date-timeline.aspx

Stakeholder schemes

Stakeholder pension schemes are designed for those people who do not have an employer, or had an employer who does not have an occupational scheme. They therefore cannot pay into an occupational scheme. If an employer does not offer an occupational scheme (many small employers are exempt) they have to arrange access to a stakeholder scheme. Employees do not have to join an occupational scheme offered by employers, instead they can join a stakeholder scheme. Likewise, self-employed people can also join a stakeholder scheme.

Stakeholder schemes have a contribution limit-this being currently £3,600 per year. Anyone who is not earning can also pay into a scheme, up to the limit above.

You pay money to a pension provider (eg an insurance company, bank or building society) who invests it (eg in shares).

These are a type of personal pension but they have to meet some minimum standards set by the government. These include:

- management charges can't be more than 1.5% of the fund's value for the first 10 years and 1% after that

- you must be able to start and stop payments when you want or switch providers without being charged

- they have to meet certain security standards, eg have independent trustees and auditors.

How much can be invested in a stakeholder pension?

There is no limit to the amount that can be invested in a stakeholder pension scheme. However, tax relief can only be obtained on contributions up to a maximum annual contribution limit (known as an individual's 'annual allowance'). For the tax year 2013/14, this is set at the lower of 100% of an individual's UK earnings or £50,000 per annum (£40,000 from 2014/15) – carry forward of unused allowances may be permitted in some circumstances. It is possible to contribute up to £3,600 per year (including tax relief) into a stakeholder pension scheme even if a person is not earning.

A member of an occupational pension scheme may also contribute to a stakeholder pension scheme.

You can start making payments into a stakeholder pension from £20 per month. You can pay weekly or monthly. If you don't want to make regular payments you can pay lump sums any time you want.

Your employer offers a stakeholder pension

The rules for stakeholder pensions changed on 1 October 2012. If you're starting a new job now or returning to one, your employer doesn't have to offer you access to a stakeholder pension scheme. they now have to offer entry through automatic enrolment.

If you're in a stakeholder pension scheme that was arranged by your employer before 1 October 2012, they must continue to take and pay contributions from your wages.

This arrangement is in place until:

- you ask them to stop
- you stop paying contributions at regular intervals
- you leave your job

If you leave your job or change to another personal pension, the money they have paid in stays in your pension pot unless you have it transferred to a different pension provider.

The range of personal pensions

Personal pensions are open to anyone, in much the same way as a stakeholder scheme. These are described more fully later on in this book.

Other ways to save for retirement
Other savings

The government offers certain tax advantages to encourage pension saving. However, the most advantageous savings plan is the Individual

133

Savings Account (ISA) discussed further on in the book. In addition, you might have regular savings accounts, your home or a second home. All of these possibilities must be factored in when arriving at an adequate retirement income.

****

22

Women and Pensions

It is a general rule that women pensioners tend to have less income than their male counterparts. Therefore, when building a retirement plan, women need to consider what steps they and their partners can take to make their financial future more secure.

Particular issues for women

These days, the rules of any particular pension scheme-whether state or private, do not discriminate between men and women. Whether male or female you pay the same to access the same level of benefits. However, this does not always mean that women end up with the same level of pension as men. This is because of the general working and lifestyle differences between men and women, for example women are more likely to take breaks from work and take part time work so they can look after family. As a result, women are more likely to pay less into a pension fund than men.

Historically, the (idealised) role of women as carers was built into the UK pensions system. Not least the state pension system. It was assumed that women would marry before having children and rely on their husbands to provide for them financially right through to retirement. As a result, women who have already retired typically have much lower incomes than men.

Changes to the state scheme for people reaching state pension age from 6th April 2010 onwards, mean that most women will, in future, retire with similar state pensions as men. However if you are an unmarried women living with a partner you should be aware of the following:

- The state scheme recognises wives, husbands and civil partners but not unmarried partners. This means that if your unmarried partner dies before you, you would not be eligible for the state benefits that provide support for bereaved dependants.

- Occupational schemes and personal pensions typically pay survivor benefits to a bereaved partner, whether married or not. However many schemes-especially in the public sector-have recognised unmarried partners only recently and, as a result, the survivor pension for an unmarried partner may be very low.

- The legal system recognises that wives, husbands and civil partners may have a claim on retirement savings built up by the other party in the event of divorce, but these will be considered along with all the other assets to be split between you and you may end up with a much lower retirement income than you had been expecting.

- The legal system does not give similar rights to unmarried partners who split up. If your unmarried partner was building up pension savings for you both, he or she can walk away with all those savings and you have no legal claim on them.

Changes to the state pension from 2016

From April 2016, the new "flat rate " state pension will typically be £155 a week, but only for those who have paid national insurance contributions (NIC's) for 35 years. Many women will not qualify, having taken career breaks to care for children.

If there are gaps in your entitlement then consider buying some added years of state pension which you can do in the run-up to retirement. The state pension purchase scheme is far more generous than any private pension, provided you live more than a few years in retirement. Be careful, though, that you're not going to be buying years that you'd actually make up through work between now and retirement, otherwise you could end up giving the government money for something you'd have got anyway.

Voluntary NIC's cost £13,90 a week or £722,80 a year, and you can normally fill gaps from the past six years. If you are due to retire after April 2016, check to see how much you will receive at gov.uk/future-pension-centre.

Have you told the government you are a carer?

The good news is that full-time unpaid carers will be entitled to the same pension as those who have worked in a paid full-time job from 2016. However, thousands of women who do not claim child benefit or carers' allowance could miss out.

These benefits signal to the Department for Work and Pensions (DWP) that an individual qualifies for NIC's. Since households earning above £50,000 are no longer eligible to claim full child benefit, many stay-at home mums may go under the radar. Similarly if women are caring for a family member but not claiming carer's allowance their unpaid work will go unrecognised. If you are a carer but don't claim any benefits pro-actively contact the DWP to report your situation. If your household income is over £50,000 you should still register for child benefit in order to receive NIC's.

****

23

The State Pension

Over 96% of single pensioners and 99% of couples receive the basic state pension. Therefore, it is here to stay. Everyone who has paid the appropriate national insurance contributions will be entitled to a state pension. If you are not working you can either receive pension credits, as discussed, or make voluntary contributions.

The basic state pension is paid at a flat rate, currently for a single person £113.10 per week. For a couple the rate is £226.20, depending on contributions (2014-15). A married couple can qualify for a higher pension based on the husband's NI contributions. If the wife has reached pension age her part of the pension is paid directly to her. If the wife is below pension age, the whole pension is paid directly to the husband.

From April 2016, the amount will change to £144 for a single person, subject to contributions, and will increase to £155-£160 over a period of four years. This is will be known as a 'flat rate' or 'single tier' system and is designed to make the current system more simple and easier to understand. Getting the flat rate however, is very much dependant on contributions.

Basic state pensions are increased each April in line with price inflation. State pensioners also receive a (£10 Christmas bonus-check current entitlement) and are entitled to winter fuel payments. Married women can claim a pension based on their spouse's NI record. Men who have reached 65 are also able to claim a basic state pension based on their wife's contribution record where the wife reaches state pension age on or after 6th April 2010.

Same sex couples, as a result of the Civil Partnerships Act 2004, along with married couples of the same sex, following the passing of the Marriage (Same sex Couples Act) in 2014, have the same rights as heterosexual couples in all aspects of pension provision.

Qualifying for state pension
How many qualifying years do you need to get the full State Pension?
The number of qualifying years you need to get a full state pension depends on when you reach your State Pension age. If you reached State Pension age before 6 April 2010, you normally needed 44 qualifying years

if you are a man, or 39 qualifying years if you are woman. If you reach State Pension age on or after 6 April 2010 but before 6 April 2016, you need 30 qualifying years. If you reach State Pension age on or after 6 April 2016, you normally need 35 qualifying years.

Using someone else's contribution record

In some circumstances, you may be able to use your husband's, wife's or civil partner's contribution record to help you qualify for a State Pension.

NI contributions counting towards a basic state pension.

Type of contribution	Paid by	Details for 2014-15
No Contributions but earnings between LEL and PT	Employees	Earning up to £111
Class 1 full rate on earnings between PT and UAP	Employees	Earnings between £153 and £805. usually paid at 12% but less if contracted out (see further on)
Class 2	Self-employed	Flat rate of £2.75 per week. Those with earnings for the year of less than £5885 can choose to opt out
Class 3	Out of the labour market and not receiving NI credits	Flat rate of £13.90 per week

Key to abbreviations
LEL = Lower earnings limit: PT = Primary Threshold: UAP = Upper Accruals Point: UEL = Upper earnings limit. LEL, PT and UEL usually increase each year UAP is fixed.

Class 1 contributions

Class 1 contributions are paid if earnings are above the primary threshold. The Threshold, set by government annually, is currently £153 per week (tax year 2014/15). If your earnings are above this set limit then you will be paying contributions at class 1 that build up to a state pension.

The level of contribution is set at 12% of earnings above the primary threshold level up to an upper earnings limit which is £805 per week in 2014/15. Contributions are paid at 2% of earnings above the upper earnings limit. If a person earns less than the primary threshold they will not pay NI contributions. The year will still count towards building up a basic state pension provided the earnings are not less than the lower earnings limit. This is £111 at 2014/15.

Class 2 contributions

Self-employed people will build up their NI contributions by paying class 2 contributions. These are paid either by direct debit or by quarterly bill at the rate of £2.75 per week (2014/15).

If profits are below the 'small earnings exception' which is £5885 in 2014/15 then there is a choice of whether or not to pay NI contributions. However, if this option is chosen, then a state pension will not be building up and there could be a loss of other benefits, such as sickness, bereavement and incapacity.

If you are a director of your own company then class 1 contributions will be paid and not class 2.

Class 3 contributions

If a person is not paying class 1 or 2 contributions or receiving HRP they can pay class 3 voluntary contributions. These are charged at a flat rate of £13.90 per week (2014/15). They can be paid up to 6 years back to make up any shortfall.

National Insurance Credits

In some situations you may get National Insurance Credits, which plug what would otherwise be gaps in your NI record. You might get credits in the following situations.

- when you are unemployed, or unable to work because you are ill, and claiming certain benefits

- If you were aged 16 to 18 before 6 April 2010, you were usually credited automatically with National Insurance credits. No new awards will be made from 6 April 2010.

- if you are on an approved training course

- when you are doing jury service

- if you are getting Statutory Adoption Pay, Statutory Maternity Pay, Additional Statutory Paternity Pay, Statutory Sick Pay, Maternity Allowance or Working Tax Credit

- if you have been wrongly put in prison

- if you are caring for a child or for someone who is sick or disabled

- if you are aged 16 or over and provided care for a child under 12, that you are related to and you lived in the UK for the period(s) of care

- if your spouse or civil partner is a member of Her Majesty's forces and you are accompanying them on an assignment outside the UK

There are special arrangements for people who worked or were detained without pay in Iraq during the Gulf Crisis. If you think you might be affected by this, write to HM Revenue & Customs (HMRC) at:

HM Revenue & Customs
National Insurance Contributions & Employer Office
Benton Park View
Newcastle upon Tyne
NE98 1ZZ
0300 200 3211

Women's state pension age is gradually increasing and when it matches the State Pension Age for men from April 2020 onwards, this type of credit will no longer be available.

The State Pension age
Currently, the state pension age is 65 for men. On 6th April 2010, the state pension age for women started to increase gradually from 60-65, to match men's. There will be further increases in the state pension age to 68 for men and women. The increase in the State Pension age is being phased in and your own particular pension age depends on when you were born. The proposed changes affect people born between April 1953 and 5th April 1960. The tables below shows the proposed retirement ages. These changes are not yet law as they need to go to parliament for approval. (For your own retirement age you should go to the Pensions Service Website).

Table 1. State pension age if woman born on or after April 6th 1950 but before April 1953

Date of Birth	Date State pension Age Reached
6th April 1951 to 5th May 1951	6th May 2012
6th May 1951 to 5th June 1951	6th July 2012
6th June 1951 to 5th July 1951	6th September 2012
6th July 1951 to 5th August 1951	6th November 2012
6th August 1951 to 5th September 1951	6th January 2013
6th September 1951 to 5th October 1951	6th March 2013
6th October 1951 to 5th November 1951	6th May 2013
6th November 1951 to 5th December 1951	6th July 2013
6th December 1951 to 5th January 1952	6th September 2013
6th January 1952 to 5th February 1952	6th November 2013
6th February 1952 to 5th March 1952	6th January 2014
6th March1952 to 5th April 1952	6th March 2014
6th April1952 to 5th May 1952	6th May 2014
6th May 1952 to 5th June 1952	6th July 2014
6th June 1952 to 5th July 1952	6th September 2014
6th July 1952 to 5th August 1952	6th November 2014
6th August 1952 to 5th September 1952	6th January 2015
6th September 1952 to 5th October 1952	6th March 2015
6th October 1952 to 5th November 1952	6th May 2015
6th November 1952 to 5th December 1952	6th July 2015
6th December 1952 5th January 1953	6th September 2015
6th January 1953 to 5th February 1953	6th November 2015
6th February 1953to March 1953	6th January 2016
6th March 1953 to 5th April 1953	6th March 2016

Table 2. Your state pension age if you are a woman and you were born on or after 6th April 1953 but before 6th December 1953.

Date you were born	Date you will reach pension age if you are a woman or the pension credit qualifying age for men and women
6th April 1953 to 5th May 1953	6th July 2016
6th May 1953 to 5th June 1953	6th November 2016
6th June 1953 to 5th July 1953	6th March 2017
6th July 1953 to 5th August 1953	6th July 2017
6th August 1953 to 5th September 1953	6th November 2017
6th September 1953 to 5th October 1953	6th March 2018
6th October 1953 to 5th November 1953	6th July 2018
6th November 1053 to 5th December 1953	6th November 2018

Table 3: Your state pension age if you are a man or a woman and you were born on or after 6th December 1953 or before 6th April 1968.

Date you were born	Date you will reach pension age if you are a woman or the pension credit qualifying age for men and women
6th December 1953 to 5th January 1954	6th March 2019
6th January 1954 to 5th February 1954	6th May 2019
6th February 1954 to 5th March 1954	6th July 2019
6th March 1954 5th April 1954	6th September 2019
6th April 1954 to 5th May 1954	6th November 2019
6th May 1954 to 5th June 1954	6th January 2020
6th June 1954 to 5th July 1954	6th March 2020
6th July 1954 to 5th August 1954	6th May 2020
6th August 1954 to 5th September 1954	6th July 2020

6th September 1954 to 5th October 1954	6th September 2020
6th October 1954 to 5th April 1968	66th birthday

Table 4. Your state pension age if you are a man or woman and you were born on or after 6th April 1968.

Increase from 66 to 67	
Date you were born	Date you will reach pension age if you are a woman or the pension credit qualifying age for men and women
6th April 1968 to 5th May 1968	6th May 2034
6th May 1968 to 5th June 1968	6th July 2034
6th June 1968 to 5th July 1968	6th September 2034
6th July 1968 to 5th August 1968	6th November 2034
6th August 1968 to 5th September 1968	6th January 2035
6th September 1968 to 5th October 1968	6th March 2035
6th October 1968 to 5th November 1968	6th May 2035
6th November 1968 to 5th December 1968	6th July 2035
6th December 1968 to 5th January 1969	6th September 2035
6th January 1969 to 5th February 1969	6th November 2035
6th February 1969 to 5th March 1969	6th January 2036
6th March 1969 to 5th April 1969	6th March 2036
6th April 1969 to 5th April 1977	67th birthday

Table 5. Your State pension age if you are a man or woman and you were born on or after 6th April 1968.

Increase from 67 to 68	
Date you were born	Date you will reach pension age if you are a woman or the pension credit qualifying age for men and women

6th April 1977 to 5th May 1977	6th May 2044
6th May 1977 to 5th June 1977	6th July 2044
6th June 1977 to 5th July 1977	6th September 2044
6th July 1977 to 5th August 1977	6th November 2044
6th August 1977 to 5th September 1977	6th January 2045
6th September 1977 to 5th October 1977	6th March 2045
6th October 1977 to 5th November 1977	6th May 2045
6th November 1977 to 5th December 1977	6th July 2045
6th December 1977 to 5th January 1978	6th September 2045
6th January 1978 to 5th February 1978	6th November 2045
6th February 1978 to 5th March 1978	6th January 2046
6th March1978 to 5th April 1978	6th March 2046
6th April 1978 onwards	68th birthday

State pensions for people over 80

From the age of 80, all pensioners qualify for an extra 25pence per week If a person does not qualify for a basic state pension or is on a low income then they may be entitled to receive what is called ' an over-80's pension' from the age of 80. For further advice concerning pensions either go to the government website www.thepensionsservice.gov.uk or refer to the list of useful leaflets at the back of this book.

Additional state pension

S2P replaced the State Earnings Related Pension (SERPS) in April 2002. SERPS was, essentially, a state second tier pension and it was compulsory to pay into this in order to supplement the basic state pension. There were drawbacks however, and many people fell through the net so S2P was introduced to allow other groups to contribute. S2P refined SERPS allowing the following to contribute:

- People caring for children under six and entitled to child benefit
- Carers looking after someone who is elderly or disabled, if they are entitled to carers allowance

- Certain people who are unable to work because of illness or disability, if they are entitled to long-term incapacity benefit or severe disablement allowance and they have been in the workforce for at least one-tenth of their working life

Self-employed people are excluded from S2P as are employees earning less than the lower earnings limit. Married women and widows paying class 1 contributions at the reduced rate do not build up additional state pension.

S2P is an earnings related scheme. This means that people on high earnings build up more pension than those on lower earnings. However, people earning at least the lower earnings limit (£111) in 2014/15 but less than the low earnings threshold (£153) in 2014/15 are treated as if they have earnings at that level and so build up more pension than they otherwise would.

Contracting out

A person does not build up state additional pension during periods when they are contracted out. Contracting out means that a person has opted to join an occupational scheme or a personal pensions scheme or stakeholder pension. While contacted out, a person will pay lower National Insurance Contributions on part of earnings or some of the contributions paid by an employee and employer are 'rebated' and paid into the occupational pension scheme or other pension scheme. This is discussed more fully further on in this book.

Increasing your state pension

There are a number of ways in which you can increase your State Pension, particularly if you have been presented with a pension forecast which shows lack of contributions and a diminished state pension. You can fill gaps in your pension contributions or you can defer your state pension. HM Revenue and Customs have a help line on 0300 123 1079 to check your record and to receive advice on whether you have gaps and how to fill them.

Filling gaps in your record

For people reaching State Pension Age on, or after, 6th April 2010, you need only 30 qualifying years for the full pension. Depending on your pension age your working life may be from 44 to 52 years. Therefore, under the post April 2010 rules, you can have substantial gaps in your record without any reduction in your basic pension.

If you wish to plug gaps in your contributions, normally you can go back 6 years to fill gaps in your record. However, if you will reach State Pension Age before April 5th 2015, special rules let you fill any gaps up to six years in total going back as far as 6th April 1975. You can make class 3 contributions to fill the gap, each contribution costs £13.90 so a full years worth costs 52 times £13.90 = £722.80 Making class three contributions can't increase your additional state pension. However Class 3 contributions do count towards the state bereavement benefits that your wife, husband or civil partner could claim if you were to die.

Deferring your state pension

Another way to boost your state pension is to delay its commencement. You can put off drawing your pension for as long as you like, there is no time limit. You must defer your whole pension, including any additional or graduated pensions and you earn an addition to the lump sum or a bigger cash sum.

In the past, if you put off drawing your own pension and your wife was getting a pension based on your NI record, her pension would also have to be deferred and she would have to agree to this. From 6th April 2010 onwards, husbands and civil partners as well as wives may be able to claim a pension based on their partners record. But a change to the rules now means that, if you defer your pension and your wife, husband or civil partner claims on your record, they no longer have to defer their pension as well.

If your pension has already started to be paid, you can decide to stop payments in order to earn extra pension or lump sum. But you can only defer your pension once. You can earn an increase in the pension when it does start of 1% for every five weeks you put off the pension. This is equivalent to an increase of 10.4% for each whole year.

Alternatively, if you put off claiming your pension for at least a whole year, you can earn a one-off lump sum instead of extra pension. The lump sum is taxable but only at the top rate you were paying before getting the lump sum. Whatever the size of the sum it does not mean that you move tax brackets.

The Pension Service, which is part of the Department of Work and Pensions publishes a detailed guide to deferring your State pension. Go to www. gov.uk-contact-pension-service.

Changes to the state pension from 2016

From April 2016, the new "flat rate " state pension will typically be £155 a week, but only for those who have paid national insurance contributions

(NIC's) for 35 years. Many women will not qualify, having taken career breaks to care for children.

If there are gaps in your entitlement then consider buying some added years of state pension which you can do in the run-up to retirement. The state pension purchase scheme is far more generous than any private pension, provided you live more than a few years in retirement. Be careful, though, that you're not going to be buying years that you'd actually make up through work between now and retirement, otherwise you could end up giving the government money for something you'd have got anyway.

Voluntary NIC's cost £13,90 a week or £722,80 a year, and you can normally fill gaps from the past six years. If you are due to retire after April 2016, check to see how much you will receive at gov.uk/future-pension-centre.

****

24

Job Related Pensions

The best way to save for retirement is through an occupational pension scheme. Employers will also contribute and pay administration costs. Schemes normally provide an additional package of benefits such as protection if you become disabled, protection for dependants and protection against inflation. Some pension schemes are related to final salary and provide a pension that equates to a proportion of salary. However, it must be said that a lot of these schemes are winding down.

Limits on your pension savings

These limits apply collectively to all private pensions (occupational schemes and personal pensions) that you may have)

Type of limit	Description	Amount
Annual contribution limit	The maximum contributions on which you can get tax relief. You can continue contributing to your 75th birthday	£3,600 or 100% of your UK relevant earnings for the year whichever is the greater
Annual allowance	The maximum addition to your pension savings in any one year (including for example employers contributions). Anything above the limit normally triggers a tax charge, but this does not apply in the year that you start to draw the pension.	Tax year 2014/15 £40,000
Lifetime allowance	The cumulative value of benefits that can be drawn from your pension savings. Any amount drawn that exceeds the limits triggers a tax charge.	Tax year 2014/15

Tax advantages of occupational schemes

The tax advantages of occupational schemes are:

- A person receives tax relief on the amount that he or she pays into the scheme
- Employers contributions count as a tax-free benefit
- Capital gains on the contributions build up tax free
- At retirement part of the pension fund can be taken as a tax-free lump sum. The rest is taken as a taxable pension

People aged 65 and over receive more generous tax allowances than younger people. Tax allowances are dealt with further on in the book.

Qualifying to join an occupational scheme

An occupational scheme can be either open to all or restricted to certain groups, i.e. different schemes for different groups. Schemes are not allowed to discriminate in terms of race or gender or any other criteria. Employees do not have to join a scheme and can leave when they wish. There might however be restrictions on rejoining or joining a scheme later on.

Not all employers offer an occupational scheme. Another pension arrangement such as a stakeholder scheme or Group Pension Scheme might be offered.

The amount of pension that a person receives from an occupational scheme will depend in part on the type of scheme that it is. Currently, there are two main types:

- Defined benefit schemes, promising a given level of benefit on retirement, usually final salary schemes
- Money purchase schemes (defined contribution schemes), where a person builds up their own savings pot. There are hybrid schemes where both the above are on offer but these are not common.

Final salary schemes

With final salary schemes, a person is promised (but not guaranteed) a certain level of pension and other benefits related to earnings. This is independent of what is paid into the scheme. Final salary schemes work well when a person stays with their employer for a long length of time or work   in   the   public   sector.

A person in such a scheme will typically pay around 5% of their salary into the scheme with the employer paying the balance of the cost which will be around 10% of salary on average. When the stock market is doing well the employer is safeguarded but when the economic climate is changing, such as at this point in time then the story is somewhat different and the employer has to pay more to maintain the level of pension. This is why such pension schemes are being withdrawn.

The pension received at retirement is based on a formula and related to final salary and years of membership in the scheme. The maximum usually builds up over 40 years. The accrual rate in such a scheme is one sixtieth or one eightieth of salary per year in the scheme.

If a person leaves the pension scheme before retirement they are still entitled to receive a pension from the scheme, based on contributions.

'Final salary' defined

The final salary is defined in the rules of the scheme. It can have a variety of meanings, for example average pay over a number of years, average of the best salary for a number of years out of ten, or earnings on a specified date. What counts are the pensionable earnings, which may mean basic salary, or could include other elements such as overtime, bonus etc.

A lump sum tax-free is included in the scheme which is defined by HMRC rules. The lump sum after 40 years of service will be around 1.5 times the annual salary.

Money purchase schemes

Money purchase pension schemes are like any other forms of savings or investment. Money is paid in and grows in value and the proceeds eventually provide a pension. The scheme is straightforward and has its upsides and downsides. The upside is that it is simple and portable. The downside is that it is related to the growth of the economy and can shrink as well as grow.

It is more difficult to plan for retirement with this kind of scheme, as distinct from the final salary scheme. As we have seen, employers prefer this kind of scheme because, although they pay into it, it doesn't place any onerous responsibilities on them.

The pension that is received on retirement will depend on the amount paid into the scheme, charges deducted for management of the scheme, how well the investment grows and the rate, called the annuity rate, at which the fund can be converted into pension. A major problem for pension schemes has been the decline in annuity rates in recent years. With most money purchase schemes the proceeds are usually given to an insurer who will administer the funds. The trustees of the scheme will choose the insurer, in most cases. In some cases, contributors are given the choice of investment. This choice will usually include:

- A with-profits basis which is a medium-risk option and which is safer and more likely to provide a good return if a person remains with the same employer. The value of the fund cannot fall and will grow steadily as reversionary bonuses are added. On retirement a person will receive a terminal bonus, which represents a chunk of the overall return
- A unit linked fund- where money is invested in one or more funds, e.g. shares, property, gilts and so on.

The cash balance scheme

A cash balance scheme lies somewhere between a final salary scheme and a money purchase scheme. Whereas in a final salary scheme a person is promised a certain level of pension at retirement with a cash balance scheme a person is promised a certain amount of money with which to buy a pension. The amount of cash can be expressed in a number of ways, for example as a percentage of salary per annum for each year of membership. So if a person is earning £50,000 per annum and the cash balance scheme is promising 15% of salary for each year of membership, there would be a pension fund of £50,000 times 15% which equals £75,000 after 10 years of membership.

Tax

Whichever type of pension that is offered, the government sets limits on maximum amounts that a person can receive. HMRC sets limits on occupational schemes which relate mainly to final salary schemes and which are shown below.

Main HMRC limits on pensions.

1. If you are in a scheme set up on or after 14th March 1989 or a scheme set up before 14th March 1989 but you joined on or after 1st June 1989, or are in a scheme set up before 14th March 1989 which you joined on or after 17th March 1987 but before 1st June 1989 if you elected to be treated under the 'post 1989 regime'.

Under the above rules you will get a percentage of final salary up to £68,000 with a limit on the lump sum at retirement of 1.5 times final salary up to a maximum of £150,000. These are the limits for the current tax year.

2. If you are in a scheme set up before 14th March 1989 which was joined on or after 17th March 1987 and before 1st June 1989 you will receive a percentage of final salary up to a maximum of 1.5 times salary or £150,000.

If you joined a scheme before 17th March 1987 you will receive a percentage of final salary up to 1.5 times salary.

Normally, the maximum pension and any other benefits build up over a long period, usually 40 years. The pension builds up at a rate of one sixtieth of final salary for each year that you are with the employer. The maximum lump sum builds up at a rate of three-eightieths of final salary.

The rules allow for a faster build up of pension if a person can't build up pension over such a long period.

The pension scheme will set a pension age, and although there used to be difference in the age at which pension was paid to men and women respectively, the dates are now usually harmonised. The most popular age for receiving pension is 65 although some opt for 60. The lowest age at which pensions can be paid is 55. In most cases, a person must give up a job before receiving an occupational pension from an employer. The rules are in the process of changing so that a pension can be received from an employer whilst still working for that employer.

Tax rules set a limit on the amount that a pension can be increased each year. This is usually inflation. If the starting pension is less than the Inland Revenue maximum then bigger increases are allowed. For pensions built up from April 6th 1997 onwards the increase is limited to a limited price indexation which means that each year the pension can be increased in line with inflation up to a maximum of 2.5% per year.

Contributions into occupational schemes

Some occupational schemes are non-contributory, which means that the employer pays all contributions. The majority of schemes, however, are contributory, with the employer and employee contributing. Usually, the employee will pay 5% of salary. With money purchase schemes the employer will also pay a specified amount of salary. With final salary schemes, which as stated are becoming less and less common, the employer will make up the balance needed to provide the specified amount. Both employer and employee will get tax relief on contributions.

Top-up schemes exist which can be used to top up pension pots but these are liable for tax in the usual way. There are two main types of top-up scheme:

- Unfunded schemes. With these schemes, an employer simply pays benefits at the time that a person reaches retirement. Income tax will be due on any benefits, even on lump sums
- funded schemes (Funded Unapproved Retirement Benefit Schemes or FURBS). This is where the employer pays contributions which build up funds to provide the eventual benefits. At the time that contributions are made they count as tax-liable fringe benefits. Usually the fund is arranged as a trust, which attracts only normal rates of tax. The benefits are tax-free when they are paid out, having been subject to tax.

If an employer runs a scheme which a person is eligible to join they must be given information about it automatically. The rules are as follows:
- an explanatory booklet must be given within two months of commencing employment if eligible to join, or within 13 weeks of joining
- each year a summary trustees report an annual accounts must be given
- employees can request a copy of the full accounts which must be provided on request
- an annual benefit statement must be provided
- options on leaving the scheme and benefit entitlements, transfer value must be provided within 3 months of request
- any announcements of changes to the scheme must be given to the scheme member within one month of the change being made

****

25

Group Personal Pension Schemes

Group personal pension schemes are a popular alternative to occupational pension schemes, particularly to smaller employers.

Group personal pension schemes are not occupational pension schemes. They are pension schemes tailored to employees of a company. The employer is not obliged to pay anything into such schemes, although many do. The amount an employer will pay is often less than an occupational pension scheme. The employee will usually end up contributing more.

Group personal pension schemes work on a money purchase basis, and, as we have seen, the employee will bear all the risks themselves. The administration charges for group personal pension schemes are usually the same as other pension funds. A plus side of group schemes is that they are seen to be particularly suitable for employees on short term contracts who cannot build up reasonable benefits in an occupational scheme because of frequent job changes. Group pension schemes are personal and travel with the employee and can be kept going without a break.

Group Personal pension Schemes and stakeholder schemes

Since October 2001, employers with more than five employees must offer at least an occupational pension scheme, a group scheme or a stakeholder scheme to employees. Stakeholder schemes are outlined further on in the book.

The pension on retirement from a group scheme will depend on the same factors as all money purchase schemes, such as the overall amount paid in and the performance of the investment. In addition, the charges taken to administer the scheme will influence the amount left in the pot.

In terms of receipt of a tax-free lump sum, group schemes are exactly the same as all other pension funds.

****

26

New Duties for Employers Relating to Provision of Pensions from 2012

From 2012, changes to pensions law affected all employers with at least one worker in the UK.

Employers need to:

- Automatically enrol certain workers into a pension scheme
- Make contributions on their workers behalf
- Register with the Pensions Regulator
- Provide workers with information about the changes and how they will affect them.

The new employer duties will be introduced in stages over 4 years, starting in 2012. Each employer will be allocated a date from when the duties will first apply to them, know as their 'staging date'. This date is based on the number of people in an employer's PAYE scheme. Employers with the largest number of employee's in their PAYE scheme will have the earliest staging date.

These staging dates can be checked on www.tpr.gov.uk/staging.

Automatic enrolment

Workers who need to be automatically enrolled are called' eligible jobholders'. An eligible jobholder is:

- Aged between 22 and the state pension age
- Working, or ordinarily working in the UK
- Earning above a certain amount (currently £10,000).

The location of the employer is not relevant when considering if the worker is an eligible jobholder. Neither is the worker's nationality or the length of their stay in the UK.

When considering whether a workers earnings are above or below the lower earnings limit, an employer needs to look at what is known as the workers 'qualifying earnings'. This will include earnings in salary, overtime, commission, bonuses, sick pay, maternity, paternity and adoption pay.

Choosing a pension scheme

Employers with an automatic enrolment duty will need to choose a pension scheme they can use for automatic enrolment. Information from the Pensions Regulator will be available to help inform this decision. Employers might use an existing scheme or set up a new one with a pension provider.

In addition, there is the National Employment Savings Trust (NEST). NEST is a pension scheme with the following characteristics:

- It has a public service obligation, meaning it must accept all employers who apply.
- It has been established by government to ensure that employers, including those that employ low to medium earners, can access pension savings and comply with their automatic enrolment duties.

Whether the scheme an employer uses for automatic enrolment is new or not, it must meet certain specific set out in legislation.

The scheme cannot:

- Impose barriers, such as probationary periods or age limits for workers.
- Require staff to make an active choice to join or take other action, e.g. having to sign a form or provide extra information to the scheme themselves, either prior to joining or to retain active membership of the scheme.

Each pension scheme will have its own rules, but all employers will need to provide the scheme with certain information about the person who is automatically enrolled.

Employers/employee contributions

Many employers offer a defined contribution scheme to staff. The rules of these schemes must require the employer to pay an overall minimum contribution of at least 8% of the workers qualifying earnings, of which at least 3% must be from the employer.

In most cases, government tax relief will account for 1% of the total 8%.

Employers who already have a pension scheme can confirm that it is suitable for automatic enrolment by a process called 'certification'.

Opt-out

Workers who have been automatically enrolled have the right to opt out of the employer's pension scheme by effectively giving one months notice. To opt out, workers must give notice via an 'opt out' notice to the employer. When employers receive a valid opt out notice within the 1-month period, they must pay back any contributions deducted from the workers pay.

Other workers

As well as automatically enrolling eligible jobholders, employers must also put certain other workers into a pension scheme, if these individuals ask. More information will be available from the Pensions Regulator later this year. Their website is www.thepensionsregulator.gov.uk.

****

27

Protecting Pensions

It is not surprising that people get very disillusioned and nervous when it comes to pensions. Since the 1980's there have been a number of scandals involving blatant theft of pensions and also incidences of mis-selling.

During the 1950's, one of Britain's biggest insurance companies, Equitable life, offered pensions which were supposed to guarantee a fixed level of income at retirement. However, by the 1990's these guarantees became too expensive and the company could not fulfill their promises. Equitable life faced many legal challenges and stopped taking on any new business. Many pensioners found themselves with poor returns and it is only now that the government is looking at compensating the victims.

In addition to theft and bad management the usual raft of 'financial advisors' mis-sold personal pensions, taking advantage particularly of the changes in the 1980's and peoples confusion. Although many people received compensation, many others did not and a lot of distress was caused to a lot of people.

To add to the above a lot of companies became insolvent and there was too little in the pension funds to fulfill pension promises. In the early days (early 2000's) there was a spate of these insolvencies and lots of people lost their pension or received less than they had planned for. The government set up several schemes to help such people and a compensation scheme was set up to assist.

The main risk to pension funds lies with occupational schemes. Although people need to be aware of changes to the state pension scheme it is safe in so far as the state is unlikely to become insolvent and unable to pay. For sure people need to keep abreast of legislation and changes to state pensions but in essence the amount promised will remain safe.

Occupational schemes

As discussed above, one of the main risks to occupational pensions is that the employer might embezzle the funds. This should be difficult given the role of the pension trustees, which will be outlined below, but it is always possible. There is also the risk that the scheme cannot pay the amount promised. This can be to do with stock market fluctuations, or, as we have all painfully seen in the last few years, a deep recession which affects people and pensions globally.

Another problem that may arise is that of schemes with defined benefits, final salary schemes, changing their rules and replacing defined benefits with less generous schemes.

Protecting pensions

Occupational schemes are usually either statutory schemes or are set up under a trust. A statutory scheme is as the name implies. It is set up under an Act of Parliament and is the usual arrangement for most public sector schemes such as police, NHS, teachers and so on. Private sector schemes are usually always set up under a trust. This ensures that the scheme is kept at arms length from the employer and business, and can't go down with the sinking ship. (Many lessons have been learned post-Mirror Group and Robert Maxwell). With a trust you will have three main elements:

- The sponsor, who will be the employer, who will initially decide on the rules of the scheme along with the benefits
- the beneficiaries, who are scheme members and any beneficiaries who might benefit if, say, a scheme member passes away
- Very importantly, the trustees who are tasked with looking after the pension fund and making sure that it is administered in accordance with the scheme rules.

The trustees are responsible for the running of the scheme but can also employ outside help, specialist help and can employ someone to administrate the scheme. They are supported in this role by the Pensions Regulator, which is the official body that regulates all worked based schemes (occupational schemes and also those personal pensions and stakeholder schemes organized through the workplace). The Pensions Regulator promotes good practice, monitors risk, investigates schemes and responds to complaints from scheme members. The Pensions Regulator has many powers, as would be expected, and can prosecute those who it thinks guilty of wrongdoing.

There is a Fraud Compensation Fund which can pay out where an occupational pension schemes assets have been embezzled or reduced because of dishonest activity. The fund is financed by a levy on all occupational pension schemes.

Other schemes

Normally, if there is a shortfall when a pension scheme is wound up, the employer would be expected to make up any shortfall. However, clearly this is not possible if the employer is insolvent and there is no money to put into a scheme. Between 1997 and 2005 some 85,000 people lost some or all of their promised pensions because of insolvency.

Because of this several schemes were set up to provide protection:

- Financial Assistance Scheme (FAS). This scheme was set up and funded by the government to provide help for those pensions scheme members in greatest need where their pension scheme started to wind up between 1st January 1997 to 5th April 2005. This is administered by the Pensions Regulator.
- Pension Protection Fund (PPF). This scheme took over from the above to provide compensation where a scheme winds up on or after 6th April 2005 with too little in the fund or an insolvent employer. In general, compensation ensures that existing pensioners carry on getting the full amount of their pension and that other scheme members get 90% of their promised pension up to a maximum limit (£36,401 at 65 in 2014-15). The PPF is financed by a levy on occupational pension schemes.
- For full details of the Pension protection fund you should go to www.pensionprotectionfund.org.uk.

Protection of personal pensions
Nearly all personal pensions come under the umbrella of the Financial Conduct Authority (FCA). In the United Kingdom, it is illegal to offer personal pensions without being authorized by the FCA. All pension providers authorized by then FCA have to go through a lot of hoops to demonstrate that they are responsible providers. The FCA oversees the activities of the Financial Services Compensation Scheme.

If a firm providing personal pensions becomes insolvent the FSCS will step in and provide compensation instead. Compensation is capped at a maximum amount, which varies according to the way that your money has been invested. Currently the maximum is £50,000 for deposits, £50,000 for investments and for long term insurance (personal pensions, life insurance and annuities 90% of the claim with no upper limit).

Complaining about pensions
State pensions
In the first instance you would deal with HMRC, regarding payment of national insurance, and also the Pension Service regarding pension forecasts. You can find details about how to complain from HMRC

website www.hmrc.gov.uk. If you have complained to the director of a particular office and you are not happy you can take your complaint to the Adjudicators Office (www.adjudicatorsoffice.gov.uk). This is an independent body that can deal with complaints about mistakes and delays, misleading advice and any other issue. In the same way you should contact the Pensions Service department dealing with pension forecasts if you have a problem in this area. If the problem carries on without resolution you can contact the Pensions Service Chief Executive.

Occupational schemes

You should initially contact the pension administrator for your scheme. If the problem is not resolved at this early stage then you should say that you want to use the formal complaints procedure, which all occupational schemes must have and must provide you with details of. If you receive no satisfaction with this process then you should contact the Pensions Advisory Service (TPAS) www.pensionsadvisoryservice.org.uk.

TPAS is an independent mediation service which will help all parties reach agreement. If this doesn't work then you can go one step further and take your complaint to the Pensions Ombudsman. You must go through TPAS before the Ombudsman will consider your complaint.

Personal pensions

You should complain first to the pensions provider. As mentioned, all firms authorized by the FSA must have a formal complaints procedure. Provided that you go down this route, and you are still unhappy, then you can complain to the Financial Ombudsman Service (FOS) www.financial-ombudsman.org.uk. It will investigate your complaint and can make orders which are binding on the firm. Where appropriate the FOS can make the firm pay you up to £100,000 to put the matter right.

****

28

Tax and Pensions

State pensions

State retirement pensions count as income for tax purposes. Tax may have to be paid if income received is high enough. The only exception to this is the £10 Christmas bonus paid to all pensioners.

State pension is paid without deduction of tax. This is convenient for non-taxpayers. For other taxpayers, the tax due will usually be deducted from PAYE or from any other pension that is received. If the tax is not deducted it will be collected through self-assessment in January and July instalments.

Occupational schemes

A pension from an occupational scheme is treated as income for tax purposes. Usually, the pension will be paid with tax deducted through the PAYE system, along with any other tax due.

Personal pensions

A personal pension will count as income for tax purposes. The pension provider will usually deduct tax through PAYE. Likewise, any other tax due will be deducted through the PAYE system. The local tax office should be contacted in order to determine individual tax positions.

Tax in retirement

When a person retires, their tax bill continues to be worked out in the usual way. However, higher tax allowances may apply so less tax is paid.

The calculations used to work out a person's individual tax bill are as follows:

- Income from all sources is added together. This includes all income with the exception of income that is tax-free.
- Outgoings that you pay in full are deducted from taxable income. 'Outgoings' means any expenditure that qualifies for tax relief.
- Allowances are subtracted. Everyone has a personal allowance. For current allowances, contact the local HMRC Office or Citizens Advice Bureau. There is a breakdown below

- What is left is taxable income. This divided into four. The first slice tax is paid at the basic rate of 20% (0-£31865) the second slice £31866-£150,000 is subject to 40% tax. The third slice is over £150,000 subject to 45% tax. (as at 2014/2015)
- Married couples allowance-this is a reduced rate allowance, given at a rate of 10% as a reduction to a person's tax bill. Married couples allowance is given only where a husband or wife were born before 6th April 1935.

Tax allowances for retirees

In the tax year 2014/15 the basic personal allowance for most people is £10,000. However, if a person is 65 or over at any time during a tax year, there will be a higher personal allowance, the age-allowance. There are two rates of age allowance: in the 2014/15 tax year the allowance is £10,500 for people reaching ages 65 to 74, and the higher age allowance is £10660 for people reaching ages 75 or more. A husband and wife can each get a personal allowance to set against their own income. See table below

Born between 6 April 1938 and 5 April 1948

Income	Personal Allowance
£0 to £26,999	£10,500
£27,000 to £27,999	Between £10,500 and £10,000. Your allowance (£10,500) goes down by £1 for every £2 that your adjusted net income's over £27,000.
£28,000 to £100,000	£10,000

Born before 6 April 1938

Income	Personal Allowance
£0 to £26,999	£10,660
£27,000 to £28,319	Between £10,660 and £10,000. Your allowance (£10,660) goes down by £1 for every £2 that your adjusted net income's over £27,000.
£28,320 to £100,000	£10,000

There is an extra allowance called a married couples allowance if you are married or in a civil partnership and either husband or wife, or both, were born before 6th April 1935. While the personal allowance saves tax at the highest rate, the married couples allowance only gives tax relief at the rate of 10% in the 2014/ 15tax year. If the husbands income is above a certain level then the married couples allowance is reduced, but never to less than a basic amount. A wife can elect to have half the basic amount of the married couples allowance (but not any of the age-related addition) set against her own income. Alternatively, the husband and wife can elect jointly for the whole basic amount to be transferred to the wife. If both partners were born after 1935, you may be able to claim marriage allowance instead. For more details go to www.gov.uk-marriage-allowance.

****

Useful addresses and websites

Association of Investment Companies (AIC)
9th Floor
24 Chiswell Street
London EC1Y 4YY
Hotline: 020 7282 5555
www.theaic.co.uk

Debt Management Office
Eastcheap Court
11 Philpot Lane
London EC3M 8UD
Tel: 0207 862 6500
www.dmo.gov.uk

Financial Ombudsman Service (FOS)
Exchange Tower
London E14 9SR
Consumer helpline: 0207 964 1000
www.financialombudsman.org,uk

Financial Conduct Authority (FCA)
25 The North Colonnade
Canary Wharf
London E14 5HS
Consumer helpline: 0300 500 0597
www.fca.org.uk

HM Revenue & Customs (HMRC)
The government department that deals
With almost all the taxes due in the UK.
Most HMRC leaflets can be obtained
From local tax offices or Tax Enquiry Centres
(look for in the phone book under `Revenue'
or `Government Department') or Jobcentre Plus offices.

International Pension Centre
The Pension Service
Tyneview Park
Newcastle upon Tyne NE98 1BA
Tel: 01912 187777
(8.00am-8.00pm,weekdays)

Investment Association
65 Kingsway
London WC2B 6TD
Tel: 020 7831 0898
www.investmentfunds.org.uk
(OEIC.S).

MoneyFACTS
www.moneyfacts.co.uk

The Pension Service
www.thepensionservice.gove.uk

Pension Advisory Service
(TPAS)
11 Belgrave Road
London SW1V 1RB
Helpline: 0300 123 1047
www.pensionsadvisoryservice.org.uk

Specialist Magazines
Money Observer
PO Box 326
Sittingbourne
Kent
ME9 8FA
01795 414820

Trade Bodies

The Investment Association
65 Kingsway
London WC2B 6TD
020 7831 0898
www.investmentfunds.org.uk

Provides information on investing in unit trusts and Oeics

Proshare Investment Clubs
5th Floor
10 Lower Thames Street
London EC3R 6AD
0203 657 7700
www.proshare.org.uk

Advises on setting up investment clubs and runs education programmes for schools on share ownership

The Association of British Insurers
61 Gresham Street
London EC2V 7HQ
020 7600 333
www.abi.org.uk
Publishes information sheets on all aspects of insurance.

The British Insurance Brokers Association
John Stow House
18 Bevis Marks
London EC3A 7JB
0870 950 1790
www.biba.org.uk

The Council of Mortgage Lenders
Bush House
North West Wing

Aldwych
London WC2B 9PJ
0845 373 6771
www. cml.org.uk

Borrowing
The National Debtline
0808 808 4000
www.nationaldebtline.co.uk

The Association of British Credit Unions
Holyoake House
Hanover Street
Manchester M60 OAS
0161 832 3694
www.abcul.org

Credit Information Agencies
Experian
Consumer help services
PO Box 7710
Nottingham NG80 7WE
0870 241 6212
www.experian.com

Equifax Europe (UK)
www.equifax.co.uk

Investment information websites

www.investment-gateway.com
www.new-online-investor.co.uk
www.find.co.uk

Index

Tracker funds, 6, 86, 95
Tradepoint, 80
Trading volume, 111

Unit trusts, 94
Unit Trusts, 45, 85

Venture capital trusts, 7, 119
Virt X, 80

With profits savings plans, 4, 42